HEADSTRONG

Also by Tim Tyrell-Smith:

30 Ideas: The Ideas of Successful Job Search

TIM TYRELL-SMITH

HEADSTRONG

THE KEYS TO A CONFIDENT AND
POSITIVE ATTITUDE DURING JOB SEARCH

Visit Tim's web site at www.timsstrategy.com

If you would like to re-print or re-purpose any of this content, please use proper attribution (Courtesy of Tim's Strategy) and provide a link back to the site (http://timsstrategy.com).

Cover design and layout: Merlina Design
http://merlinadesign.com

 **Creator, Blogger, Speaker at Tim's Strategy™**

Tim Tyrell-Smith is a 22 year veteran consumer packaged goods marketing executive. Passionate about ideas and strategy, Tim lives with his wife and 3 children in Mission Viejo, California.

This book is dedicated to my wife, Michele, who has supported me throughout this journey with love and patience. And a friendly dose of sarcasm.

Contents

Preparing For A Big Interview Day

There Will Be Tough Days

Momentum Can Be Elusive

The Final Stretch

Introduction

In 2008 I started a blog called Spin Strategy. Its purpose was to share my ideas and strategy with the job search community. Having successfully finished my own job search a few months earlier, it felt right to spend some time giving back

But once I started writing, I couldn't stop. The feedback from readers was awesome and it seemed I was helping quite a few people succeed in their process. And that felt really good. I also received feedback that a lot of the ideas applied beyond job search. So in January 2010, I expanded the scope of the blog and changed the name:

Tim's Strategy™
Ideas For Job Search, Career and Life

And it has been a blast to stay a part of people's lives well beyond the end of their job search. Helping them succeed in their careers and lead a more fulfilling life.

In 2010 I also published my first book. It was a free e-book that we put into print. So that those uncomfortable with downloads or those wanting a physical book in their lap could have one. *30 Ideas: The Ideas of Successful Job Search* is my summary book of many ideas shared on the blog in the first year and a half.

That book includes a section (10 chapters) on the psychology of successful job search. And because I believe so much on the importance of a positive psychology in job search, I wanted to dedicate a whole book on this subject.

Some of the content for this book comes from the blog. Much of it comes from a presentation I've given time and time again. *"It's All In Your Head: The Psychology of Successful Job Search"* is the name of the presentation. And I love sharing it with job seekers.

Why? It resonates. It helps. And it encourages.

So this book is here as a guide to help you build and maintain a confident and positive attitude throughout your job search. It is written in a "what to expect at each stage" method so that you can grab bits and pieces wherever you are in your job search process.

At the end of each chapter, you'll find three discussion questions to help you apply the ideas from each chapter. I hope you find those helpful.

I wish you all the best in your search. Finding a job can be a difficult and frustrating process. Especially when it continues beyond your expectation.

Perhaps this book can be something to lean on when times get hard.

Tim Tyrell-Smith, March 2011

The Importance Of A Confident And Positive Attitude

1

Why Your Attitude Is So Critical

It is our attitude at the beginning of a difficult task which,
more than anything else, will affect its successful outcome.
William James

It really matters.

**Next to having a solid strategy during job search, your
attitude is critically important to your effort.**
What do I mean by attitude exactly? I mean the activity that's happening in your mind and the link to specific behaviors it carries out
on your behalf.

And when is it most important during job search? Well, it's hard to
imagine a time when it is not critical. But let's say that all is probably
working better in the beginning. Mostly. In that your early days tend
to be filled with a bit of extra confidence.

And some of us are optimistic in those early days. That can lead to
complacency. In other words, the brain takes in the environment and
says: "We're good." And instead of aggressively building a network,
we ride the early waves hoping they'll take us to shore.

So why exactly is your attitude so critical during job search?

Every Action You Take
- If you are hurt or angry about a lay-off.
- If you are brimming with confidence after a week of small victories.

• If you are frustrated with a lack of response from an employer.

So before you sit down to write or update your resume, pay attention to how you are feeling about that task. About your personal brand.

There are better days than others to complete certain tasks.

Before you pick up the phone to call that important new networking contact, be aware of your confidence meter. That call needs to be made by a "strong you". Not the "tentative you" or "selfish you". And before you walk into a networking event, take a personal inventory and make sure you are all there. Ready to be interesting. Upbeat. And full of smiles.

Every Reaction You Have To Events

Let's remember that job search is an up and down time in life. And while we never want to expect bad news, it will come at some point to most of us. Someone will disappoint you along the way.

"Sometimes the road does not rise up to meet your feet."

So you have be prepared for the possibility that there will be bad days. Not "expecting them to the point that you stop thinking positive", but having an open mind and a structured mind-set ready to go. When the days arrive. That way your reaction is:

"Yep, Tim said there would be days like this. Now, how do I work through it and build a plan for next week's effort?"

I think there is value in recognizing those bad days or weeks. Come up with a name for them (e.g. Gremlins).

There are also slow days or weeks when absolutely nothing happens. Dead time. So in addition to having a plan for reacting to the bad days, you need to be ready for the slow days.

"Kind of like a snow day."

I wrote up a nice long list once of 101 (other) things you can do during your job search (see chapter 38). One or two of these might help you on an upcoming snow day.

The Way You Treat Others

How would you grade yourself as a fellow job seeker? Are you open to new friendships? Are you willing to share leads? Do you only talk to the people who can help you?

Of course some of this has to do with who you are in a larger sense. How you were brought up. And potentially your level of relational intelligence (your ability to relate with compassion). But I will also tell you that a confident and prepared person treats others differently.

"Being confident allows your "self" to come out and play."

Like the small child that hides behind mom's legs when meeting a new person. You smile more. You speak up when giving your elevator pitch to a room of 50 people. You are more interesting.

The Way Others React To You

If someone mistreats you or dismisses you. Your can have one of two reactions.

1. You can internalize it. Finding a number of ways to blame yourself for what happened.

2. You can shine a big bright light on it. Figure out objectively what happened and move on.

Perhaps you did something you shouldn't have done. Perhaps the other person misspoke or handled something in a way that you did not expect.

Learn something from the experience and move on. But you have to move on. And your attitude is critical in your ability to do so.

So, let me say that this is not easy some days. I have been where you are and I remember my bad days. I remember not always reacting to situations in the perfect way each and every time.

And I remember how I felt on those days. So the focus is on paying attention. To what is happening in your mind.

And how your behavior is reflecting it back onto the world around you.

CHAPTER DISCUSSION QUESTIONS

1. How is your attitude this week?

2. Where would you put your confidence level on a scale of 1-5?

3. What happens to you when you're not feeling 100%?

2

Losing A Job That Really Matters

I never could stand losing. Second place
didn't interest me. I had a fire in my belly.

Ty Cobb

If you have a job that makes you especially proud. Gives you confidence. And a significant role in the community.

What would you do if you lost that job? Maybe you did.

And it doesn't have to be your day job. Because for some people, their most valued job is not the one that they work from 8-5, but the one that keeps them away from home a few nights a week. Being on the board of a local charity or your son's little league.

But for many it is that day job. It is all they have known and all they've been known for throughout their career.

In fact, they are so tied up in that job they can't imagine doing something else or being introduced as someone else.

Did this happen to you? Or a friend of yours?

If so, you know that this can be one of the toughest lay-off or firing experiences.

"Someone has taken away your identity."

Perhaps something you were passionate about in life. The platform you stood upon.

And those first few weeks at home after leaving your position can be miserable. Not just the shock and awe of the experience (like a tornado just hit) but also the slow realization that this role was tied directly to your social life. And now your career path, it appears, has just been interrupted.

And for some this platform (your job) was powerful enough that people returned your calls the same day. With an urgency to see what you needed. And now they don't because you lost your platform. That job or role in life that helped you stay up above others on the priority list. And now they don't.

But it doesn't have to be that way.

You can start now. To create a new platform for your life and career. One that is not reliant on one day job or one volunteer role to keep you afloat in case of emergency.

How?

Start by writing down the events, people, projects, and places that matter in your life.

> "Where are you currently finding your joys, sense of purpose and sense of belonging?"

If your list is really short. Or if your list is long but centered on one big role that really defines you.

Then I think you need to rebuild your platform. To establish a broader focus in life. So that if one of the supports is removed, you will remain afloat.

I can hear some of you saying that you don't have time to build a bigger platform. That with a day job, house and kids, there's no time for anything else.

But I think there's always time for something you care about. Maybe it is a passion or a pursuit. One less hour of TV a night can be the time you read books on the subject. And waking up one hour earlier can get you working before the kids wake up.

CHAPTER DISCUSSION QUESTIONS

1. Have you ever lost a job that was really important to you?

2. How do you replace a work community during job search?

3. What can you build in and around your life to prevent the removal of that one thing destroying a big part of you?

3

A Stable Career And Life Platform

To put it bluntly,
I seem to have a whole superstructure with no foundation.
But I'm working on the foundation.

Marilyn Monroe

As we discussed in the last chapter, if your job is the main source of pride in your life, the bulk of your socializing, the only potential means of making money and the only place where you focus your creativity, then you are at risk. At risk of being hit especially hard if you were to lose that job.

So my goal here, whether you are working or looking, is to get you thinking about building a more stable career and life platform. One that is balanced enough to allow some change without completely upending your life.

Many talk about the desire for a "stable job" when looking for work.

Think bigger and you can build stable career and life.

And here are the five ways:

Create An Opportunity For Multiple Incomes

If you have more than one way of making money in your life, it adds stability. No question. And the goal here isn't to have a second full time job. It could be one or two things on the side that contribute something to your vacation fund. Or it could be the seeds for a different career altogether. One that is not reliant upon someone else.

This will take time to develop and will certainly not generate a big income right away, but you are looking to give yourself a few other options. And there is a psychological value here as well.

"Instead of feeling totally ruined after a lay-off, you have only lost one piece of your puzzle."

And you can conduct your job search with perhaps a little more confidence knowing that your platform is still floating.

Further, by trying some new career paths in a small way, you get a sense of what it feels like to do that job, to see whether people will pay you for it and find out if it is really a path to wealth (not a hole in which to bury savings).

You can create a product of your own (a book, jewelry, a blog, a better mouse trap) or a service (business consulting, interior design, social media). It will take time, yes. But as I said in the prior chapter, we all have a few hours a day to develop something else in life. Even if it doesn't feel like it.

Bring A Known Hobby To Life

This is related to way #1 but for a different reason. The goal here is not to make money. It is to focus your creativity to another significant place in your life.

"To create another source of pride and confidence."

Yours could be music, digital photography, gardening, scrap booking, writing, cooking and the like. So that if your day job is threatened, your first reaction won't be "I'm sunk" but rather "Looks like I'll have some more time to (your hobby) over the next few months!"

Well developed hobbies help to provide added dimension to our lives by associating our feeling of self worth with something we love and can do whether the day job is there or not.

Find A Place To Give Back

Identifying a unique need in your community and filling it with your abilities, can be very rewarding.

But this is about creating more of a lifelong commitment to an organization that matters to you. A church, a soup kitchen, a community center, a school, a charity or special event in your town.

This one, in fact, is one of the key ways you can shift your focus away from a career-centered life to one also centered on the needs of your community. Bob Buford writes about this in his book Halftime – Changing Your Game Plan From Success To Significance. Shifting your focus in life toward having an impact on the world. Not just your or your company's bottom line.

More Time With Family And Friends

Some of us work too much. And many of us think too much about work even when we are not there. So you become it. And when a lay off comes, the effect is global because that role you lost had permeated your life.

Like a sponge on a plate of water, that darn job sucked up every ounce of time and focus. And your social life suffered.

It is what you talked about at parties, at little league games and at the gym. And your friends and family are tired of hearing about your job.

But I'll bet you are a lot more interesting than the experiences provided by your day job. And I'll bet your friends and family would love to hear about other parts of your life. Your re-focus will insulate you in a job loss situation since you will have a social life at home and in your community that rivals or outpaces your social life at work.

It is great to have friends at work. But those friendships are not always as strong as you think. If you've ever been laid off, you know that work friendships are largely reliant upon your working at that company. Because they are built on shared work experiences. Of course, the real friends there you'll keep. But most will re-focus their attention to other co-workers. Instead of you.

Create A Financial Safety Net

This is the advice that is hard to hear. And it is even harder to do. Many of us struggle to fund a 401k much less build a savings account. But the truth is that if you have money in the bank or access to money via a low interest credit line, you can relax just a bit knowing that a job loss is not catastrophic. That you have some time to figure this whole thing out.

Money acts to stabilize a key life concern. And helps to build a solid platform. It also enables some of the other ideas above. In case a small investment will let you kick off a hobby, give back to the community or start a side business while you are working a day job.

So I hope that at least one of these five ways will help to stabilize your life and career. To find more ideas on this concept and a deeper discussion on becoming someone of significance, be sure to read chapter 17 on ways to become a person of influence. It includes a lot of great examples of people who have done it successfully.

CHAPTER DISCUSSION QUESTIONS

1. How have you found ways to balance your personal and work life?

2. Do you have a stable platform?

3. If not, which of these ideas above will you pursue?

4

Keep Your Head Above Water

"May the road rise up to meet you, may the wind be ever at your back. May the sun shine warm upon your face and the rain fall softly on your fields. And until we meet again, May God hold you in the hollow of his hand."

Irish Blessing

In life and in job search, the road does not always rise up to meet you. Sometimes the road drops off and becomes a ditch. And you are left there. Legs dangling.

Your ability to react with perspective when it happens is key to maintaining a positive attitude.

How is it that you can have a great week and then one piece of bad news on Friday ruins the weekend?

And the truth is that experiencing, dealing with and learning from disappointment is good for you. It prepares you for bigger disappointments down the road. Makes the smaller ones seem, well, small. And they will come again. Especially if you are trying to build something. Trying to do something important. Like finding that next great role in your career.

"But what should keep you going is the larger mission."

What's your larger mission and how can you keep that in the center of your thinking?

Meeting with job seekers every week keeps me in tune with the real issues out there. The disappointments.

Through one-on-one's and networking events here in Southern California, e-mail exchanges, phone calls and resume reviews with folks around the U.S. and around the world, I get a first hand look at what's bugging you.

And then I can write about it – offering a few ideas to help.

So I say all this to let you know that I remember the ups and downs from my search back in 2007.

- I remember feeling let down after not getting the answer from a company that I wanted (or thought I wanted).
- I remember the air leaving my lungs when I returned home from a two-day trip and not a single e-mail had arrived relating to my search.
- I remember getting into a real funk when my expectations were not met days or weeks after a "great interview"

When I meet with job seekers today, I hear those same emotions coming out. Sometimes it shows as frustration. Sometimes stress or anger. And, every once in a while, just a sense of loss.

So I try to help define that larger mission for them.

> **"The big picture that helps them to see a single piece
> of bad news in a new or brighter light."**

The same light I shine on my own disappointments.

CHAPTER DISCUSSION QUESTIONS

1. What kind of ups and downs are you experiencing each week?

2. How do you cope with bad news?

3. How could you put those bad days in perspective and learn something?

Your Transition Begins

5

Lay-Off, Fired or Leaving On Your Own

To improve is to change; to be perfect is to change often.
Winston Churchill

There are many ways to leave a job. Some are positive and productive. And some are cruel. Frustrating and bewildering.

Some of us are victims of the man. True innocents Others are victims of mistakes we've made all on our own. Or simply lacking the smarts, to remove ourselves from a bad situation when we still could. Under our own power.

Being aware of your mind-set as you begin a job transition is critical. When your mind is positive, negative or somewhere in between, this will dictate the way you play with others. Especially if you lost a job that really mattered.

Layoffs
For the most part, getting laid-off stinks. It is often without warning. In fact, getting laid off is like experiencing a tornado. And there is a definite re-building process that needs to happen as job search begins. Physically and mentally.

But some who experience layoffs have an early epiphany that perhaps their termination was not such a bad thing. They see it as a fresh start. A chance to transition to something new. To meet new people and experience a new company's culture.

For others, any benefit from layoffs comes later. Often much later. Early on, though, there is a strong feeling of abandonment. Separation from the company that nurtured you. Provided comfort, friendships and a sense of work happiness.

"You didn't just lose a job. You lost a community. A culture."

And there's pain in realizing that the community is still working without you. That your participation was optional. That's a hard pill to swallow.

Especially if you felt you gave your life to that company. The layoffs came. And they decided to drop you at the curb.

Fired

Getting fired can be brutal. And it really carries some different implications. When layoffs come, you are usually a part of a larger scale change in the organization. You are not a bad person. You are just being swept up.

Getting fired is personal. It says that you are less than average. Or that you did something wrong. Damaged goods. No matter the actual reason for your firing, there are some different questions in your head. Things you need to process before you can travel to interview land or begin career networking for the job search.

Because when someone asks how you became available, you have to prepare a story. Or at least a version of one. That doesn't shrink completely from the truth. Yet allows you to tell it without feeling like a pariah.

And here there is a need to base your story in truth.

"Part of telling your story is coming to grips with it."

Recognizing that mistakes were made or that the fit wasn't entirely good. Or as good as you thought when you first accepted the original job offer.

Leaving On Your Own

If you quit your job or are planning to quit your job before you find another, you are sitting on a very different set of ideas and certainly fewer inhibitions. If you've done it or are thinking about doing it, you really need to think through that decision.

Because it is a big one. One that I made after months of deep thought. I decided to leave to pursue a big passion. Helping others. Something I felt I had to do. And saw my mid-40's as the right time to do it.

"In the end, your job is to know yourself."

To know your mind-set. And your influencing experiences.

Before you transition and begin engaging the job search community.

CHAPTER DISCUSSION QUESTIONS

1. How did you leave your last job?

2. If you wrote a note to your last manager, what would you say?

3. Who could you talk to about your feelings after being laid off?

6

Welcome To Humanity

*"My humanity is bound up in yours,
for we can only be human together."*
Desmond Tutu

There really is no way around it. Sorry to break it to you. But if you decide that career networking is either right or necessary for you right now, you'll have to come to grips with the following fact:

"The social networking crowd is an interesting bunch."

And so if you do venture out to the great networking halls of the world. Get ready.

You will meet them all. Whether that appeals to you or not. Because, as in life, you will kiss a few frogs on the way to the ball. The good news is that you will get to the ball. And you will kiss a prince or princess when you get there.

Whatever your fancy.

And why am I telling you this? Well, whether you are new to social networking or a veteran, it always helps to be reminded that we are all in this thing together.

As you head out for an evening of "get to know", you will meet them - good or bad, shy or outgoing, happy or sad, prepared or lost, confident or scared - and each needs something from you.

Yes, you will meet all types. And you can guess that there are more types that can be properly counted.

So I try to keep it simple with the diagram from above. At least for today, there are givers and takers. And luckily for each of us, the tide has shifted.

This economy has brought out the best in us. Even the most callous seem to want to give back. Or are at least open to it.

So we're all in this together. It's true. But on a more practical level, there's another reason you need to hear this.

In order to successfully navigate the social networking world, you will need to introduce yourself to and interact with this incredibly diverse crowd.

Are you ready to do that?

Do you want to do that? Do you have what it takes to be a giver?

So now I hope you feel prepared. Prepped to meet some really smart people, some who are still learning. And, unfortunately, a few who will never get it.

Yes, you have to meet them too. Sorry.

CHAPTER DISCUSSION QUESTIONS

1. How are you reacting to the job search community?

2. Who out there needs your help with networking?

3. Who could you reach out to for help with your situation?

7

The Average Job Seeker

*"I am only an average man but, by George,
I work harder at it than the average man."*
Theodore Roosevelt

Are you average? Are you living in the middle of the pack? If so, let's make a change. Let's decide that this job search is going to be the one where you move from average to "better". Better educated. With a larger network and a more confident attitude.

Interested?

**The average job seeker (and those living below average)
will spend more time looking for their next role.**

And it will be harder. But being average is not about your IQ, your college education, your last job income or even your leadership skills.

So can we get everyone above average? No. But perhaps we can raise the average to a point where everyone is at least using the tools available. And each has the opportunity to climb the job search and networking ladder.

To a better place.

So, what defines the average job seeker? The diagram shows four indicators from my experience that suggest that you are like most others out there looking.

Now, everyone's first reaction to each are different. Some will feel instantly attached to all four saying: "Yes, I have work to do". Some will feel intimidated saying: "Yes, I heard that I need to do better with all this, but how?" And others will look past them all saying "Not me".

So, let's talk about each of these categories...

A Limited And Local Network

If you have established specific and tangible job search objectives, (Chapter 9) what kind of a network have you built to support them? Most job seekers know far too few people. And those that they do know are often missing from their LinkedIn 1st level connections. Why? They haven't asked.

- **Is your network limited?** Who do you know? And who have you taken the time to meet? To get to know. If you have fewer than 100 first level connections on LinkedIn. Fewer than 50. You have some work to do. If you are networking via computer instead of in person. And if you are not out there exposing your candidacy to the world.

- **Is your networking local?** Well, for some of you, this might make sense. You have decided that your career will remain in Hong Kong, Tampa Bay or London. And no force of nature will move you. Even an extended job search. But for those of you looking beyond your current city or those of you who have decided that a relocation would be OK. What are you doing to extend your network beyond your current city? Of course it's not easy to network with people in a far away city. But there are ways...

Not Social Media Savvy

Now I'm not here to berate you about your lack of social media skills. I'm really not. I'm just saying that social media skills can be a difference maker. The difference in the way you are found, perceived and the way your candidacy is re-distributed to the larger job search community.

And if you are one of those still falling back on the "not for me" crutch, I'll keep asking you to give it a try. At least get yourself established on Linkedin, Twitter and Facebook. The people that know you, care about you and are ready to help you are out there waiting. Some just haven't met you yet.

No Established Personal Brand

Who are you? What about your method to get things done gets you noticed? And what experiences define the impact you'll have on a future company?

Now ideally you've been working to establish your brand with a focused effort. Throughout your career. But if you are like most people, you are building it out of necessity. Everyone keeps asking: what are your strengths? So, if you haven't established a personal brand, it is not too late.

Initially Confident

Many job seekers begin their job search effort with confidence. While they've heard it is a tough market, they see themselves as different. After all, finding a job has never been difficult before, right?

And, really, everyone has at least two hot leads right away. One of those two will likely pan out you say. But if it doesn't, where have you left yourself?

This is where we learn about two enemies of success in job search. Ones that the average job seeker runs into at full speed. I've shared the danger of optimism and the problems that come with procrastination. Avoid them and you will steer clear of complacency. And a stalled job search.

So let's raise the average together. By all being a bit smarter. A bit more efficient. By being a proactive supporter of each other.

Being average in job search is a choice. Choose to be better.

CHAPTER DISCUSSION QUESTIONS

1. Are you average?

2. Which of the above characteristics best describes you?

3. What action could you take today to improve?

8

How To Prepare For And Thrive In Tough Times

"Back of every mistaken venture and
defeat is the laughter of wisdom, if you listen."
Carl Sandburg

It may be that there's not a lot you can do. Whether you are a fan of nature or nurture, you have been built from the ground up. To either succeed during tough times. Or scramble through them as best you can.

Based on your prior years experience, you've come into your present self with either a waterfall of confidence, a slow drip or something in between. But you can start to fix that.

How do you measure your flow?

If you look back on your last career transition or if you are experiencing one now, you are likely well aware of just how bullish you feel about your ability to land on your feet.

Or you may have started questioning whether the core ability to succeed in tough times is hard wired in you.

But I don't question that. Because I've done it already. And because I have, I know I can do it again.

How?

Here are my examples:

- My parents divorced during my last year of high school. Splitting up our family and forcing me into being an adult sooner than I planned.
- My dad lost his job during my freshman year of college. It forced me to get two jobs to stay enrolled and housed.
- I completed an MBA while working full time.
- My wife and I had twins. And a two year old. At the same time.
- I signed up for and completed a marathon in just over 4 hours. That was hard.
- I built a website and blog part time. Sacrificing family time and sleep. Because I loved doing it.

Each of these examples has now become part of my experience. Experiences that I draw on when times get tough.

The knowledge that I have made it through successfully is a powerful piece of evidence that I can do it.

Time and time again.

Now I'll ask you. What does your list of life experiences look like? And how do you tap into that experience when you are challenged in life?

Have a short list? Then start creating those experiences. Right now.

Pick one thing in your life that you know will be hard and set out to do it. Climb a mountain, run a half-marathon, start a networking group, go back and get that degree.

Because once you finish, you can add that to your list. And tap that extra confidence when you need it. And, soon, you can add "successful job search in the worst economy ever". While staring "tough times" right in the eye

CHAPTER DISCUSSION QUESTIONS

1. What experiences do you have getting through tough times?

2. What does your experience say about you?

3. How can you apply that knowledge to your job search?

The First Things To Do

9

Create Specific Job Search Objectives

"Many people flounder about in life because they do not have a purpose, an objective toward which to work."

George Halas

There is one question job seekers struggle to answer. It baffles me. How such a simple question throws off so many.

And then it doesn't baffle me. Because I've been through a job search. And I meet with job seekers every week and see their brains working as the answer is being generated. And I know at least one reason why people struggle.

It is a question that I have never seen someone answer to my satisfaction. Without some prodding.

Isn't it the most basic question someone could ask a job seeker? One that signifies an offer of help. A window of opportunity. One which most job seekers stumble over.

"The question: What are you looking for?"

How do you answer this question?

And just to cut to the quick, here's the answer I'm looking for when I ask it: "I am looking for a director level position in apparel sales based on the West Coast. My target companies include Nike, Under Armour, Adidas."

These are what I affectionately call your job search objectives. It tells me specifically what "you are looking for" and gives me what I need to help you.

(I'll tell you how to choose and penetrate your target companies in chapters 14 and 15.)

Without this level of detail, I am stuck with vague generalities.

Such as:"I'm looking for a job in sales with a stable company. I can do high tech, aerospace or medical devices."

But in reality most answers I get to this question are nowhere near this short. They tend to meander. Like someone talking as they walk through a maze built out of hay bails. And when they finally make it out of the maze, well, they've lost me.

And I blame this on two things:

Poor preparation

Either you have not written specific objectives or you have not practiced sharing them in public. If you've not written them, you can practice by answering questions as part of submitting your objectives to my Watchlyst™ on timsstrategy.com.

Which you can do today. Even if you don't hit the "submit" button, you can use the process to determine if you are ready to share them with others.

Purposeful avoidance

Many I meet during their job search are vague on purpose. Because in their mind, being too specific means that you are pulling yourself off of the general job market.

**"That the creation of specific objectives
means that you will get fewer job leads."**

And this part is true. But job search is not about how many leads you get. It is about the quality of leads and their fit with what you want to do next in your career. And they should be coming from people who have tangible (easy to remember) information about you.

You may have other reasons to not have specific objectives. A warning: I won't like those either.

CHAPTER DISCUSSION QUESTIONS

1. What are your specific job search objectives?

2. What is holding you back from writing down specifics?

3. Who should you be communicating these objectives to each week?

10

Write Your Positioning Statement

*"If you've earned a position, be proud of it. Don't hide it.
I want to be recognized. When I hear people say, 'There's
Joan Crawford!' I turn around and say, 'Hi! How are you!'"*

Joan Crawford

If you are a regular blog reader and have used a few of the free job search tools, you may have seen me reference the term "positioning statement".

I suggest you put it on your resume as well as on your SoloSheet™ Networking Bio and FlashCard™ Business Card. Before I show an example of a positioning statement, let me get you clear on the concept of positioning.

As a young marketing guy starting my career, I bought many books. Books that would help speed my ascension into marketing lore. Or at least keep me from looking silly in the big conference room.

One of the books that really led the way for me was written by Al Ries and Jack Trout called Positioning: The Battle For Your Mind. Originally penned in 1981, it describes:

"How to be seen and heard in the overcrowded marketplace."

Does that sound like the job market?

So positioning yourself makes sense. It's not just some harebrained task I thought of to keep you busy!

In the book, the authors walk us through the perils of a busy society. One that gets millions of advertising messages everyday. And maybe, just maybe, only opens its ears for messaging that is well planned, well written, and strikes a particular or differentiating chord.

According to the authors:

> "The basic approach to positioning is not to create something new and different, but to manipulate what's already up there in the mind, to re-tie the connections that already exist."

How about a positioning statement example, you say?

Well, one of the most compelling in the book is the re-positioning of Milk Duds candy. A product stuck in the mind of consumers as a mere movie house snack. One eaten by an older, more sophisticated crowd. Ten year olds.

A ten year old (back then) had a small income – their allowance – and other candy bars were consumed too quickly. Before the movie even started! Since chocolate alone melts in your mouth more rapidly, an opportunity existed. So Milk Duds could become "The Long Lasting Candy Bar" due to its caramel center. Better value on a short budget and lasts all movie long.

Milk Duds already had that feature, the company just wasn't talking about it. It also, by definition, re-positioned the competition as "short lasting".

So, positioning yourself in job search requires an important task.

"To define your candidacy as simply and clearly as possible."

So I suggest nothing more than a four to six word statement. It defines your role, your worth and establishes a place (or position) in the mind of a hiring manager, HR person, recruiter or networking contact. Think about it as your tag line (e.g. Avis: We try harder).

Here are a few positioning statement examples to get you started:

Classically Trained Consumer Marketing Executive

Customer-Driven Service And Parts Technician

Strategy and Data Powered Sales Manager

Brand Building Product Management Professional

Growth-Oriented Chief Financial Officer

Problem Solver and Detail Oriented IT Manager

Each of these statements says something about you. Something you can and should reinforce in your professional resume (accomplishments) and in your interviews (tangible examples). It represents who you are and what you will bring to your new role.

CHAPTER DISCUSSION QUESTIONS

1. So what will you use to define your position in this crowded market?

2. What should go on a list of what makes you unique?

3. How can you incorporate these words throughout your marketing materials?

11

Create a Killer Elevator Pitch

"Give a girl an education and introduce her properly into the world, and ten to one but she has the means of settling well, without further expense to anybody"

Jane Austen

In my 30 Ideas book, I included a chapter to help you deliver a great elevator pitch to your local networking group. Because when your elevator pitch has a pitch problem, you won't have the impact. And no one will rush the stage to meet you when it is over.

And I think that one of the most important results of a good elevator pitch is that people want to come find you. To introduce themselves. And network with you.

A great concept, right?

Here's my advice on how to create the pitch that everyone will love.

Six easy steps.

Step 1 - Tell us your name...

Good morning, my name is Tim Tyrell-Smith

Step 2 - Tell us your positioning statement (four to six words that uniquely define you in the market)

I am a "classically trained marketing executive and brand builder"

Step 3 - Tell us your brief career summary (last position, industry, a key accomplishment or two)

My expertise is consumer goods – primarily food – with additional experience in computer and automotive accessories. My last position was Director of Marketing with Meguiar's Car Wax where I helped the company achieve its first ever #1 market share position.

Step 4 - Tell us your work philosophy (how you work, what reinforces your true value)

I believe in a fix, build and drive strategy. This includes removing any "growth stoppers" before investing in new products or marketing.

Step 5 - Tell us your specific job search objectives (target title, function, industry, geography, companies)

I am looking for a VP Marketing role in a small to mid-size consumer goods company located in Southern California. My target companies include Black & Decker, Hansen's, Langer's Juice and Pepsi Bottling.

Step 6 - Tell us how you can help others (i.e. us)!

I would love to meet with others interested in consumer goods or marketing careers. Glad to help anyone with my connections!

And that's it! About 45 seconds. You can add or delete words to get down to 30 or up to 60 depending on the guidelines provided by your networking group.

Know you know how to create one. Think you can do it? I'll bet you can.

CHAPTER DISCUSSION QUESTIONS

1. How would you rate your current elevator pitch?

2. What one takeaway do you want to deliver for your audience?

3. Can someone send you targeted job leads based on your pitch?

12

Write Great Accomplishment Statements

"It had long since come to my attention that people of accomplishment rarely sat back and let things happen to them. They went out and happened to things."

Leonardo da Vinci

Writing a great accomplishment statement is just the beginning of the conversation about you. It is the result of a story you should be telling in your marketing documents.

"Stories that illustrate your impact in the world."

So there's a bigger story. And there's an element of passion. An energy about your great works in prior companies. And the better you do this, the better a hiring manager can envision you doing similar things for their department or company.

And the accomplishment statements you write are your way to engage the reader. So that you will be granted an interview. An audience to tell your stories in more detail and share your energy.

So they have to be good. Well written. They also have to be relevant and measurable. And remember not to mix them up with your responsibilities.

So to help you think about how to write a great accomplishment statement, I thought I would illustrate an example for you. And then walk you through each part. Here it is:

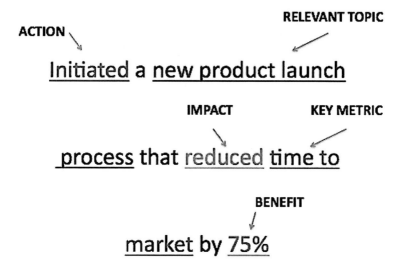

So now to take you through it step-by-step:

Action

There's a great list of action verbs at Quint Careers (http://www.quintcareers.com/action_skills.html). You can use a few of those or think up your own. But make sure that your leading words suggest movement, ownership and leadership.

Relevant Topic

What does your target company care about? What do you know about the role you will play? With a solid knowledge of your likely audience, you can focus on the right topics.

Impact

You need a word here that clearly states what happened. In this case, something got reduced. And that is a good thing. Make sure the positive impact you had is clearly stated.

Key Metric

What was impacted? Make sure that metric is also relevant and measurable in the way your industry defines it. In an economy where budgets are heavily scrutinized, your ability to measure and report will be important. No matter what your role is in the company.

Benefit

Accomplishment statements need numbers. Something tangible like a % increase/decrease, $ revenue up or $ cost down. And you can strengthen the benefit by adding a second short sentence to answer the "so what" question. In this case, you could add: "BENEFIT: Delivered new revenues 6 months sooner than expected." That's a nice surprise.

So what if you charted out your key accomplishments like this? Sound like a lot of work? I'll bet if you do it for a few, you'll get the idea. And have this structure in your mind as you write or re-write the rest.

CHAPTER DISCUSSION QUESTIONS

1. What are your favorite action words?

2. What is the benefit of each of your accomplishments?

3. If you ask, "so what?" at the end of each, can you answer?

13

How To Tell Great Stories

"If history were taught in the form of stories,
it would never be forgotten."

Rudyard Kipling

Great stories get us interested. They help us become linked into a topic. They include important context and background so we better appreciate what happens at the end. And best of all, a great story is often shared with others.

But many of us struggle telling stories, especially when the topic is our life and our career. Learning to do this well can positively affect the outcome of an important job interview.

So what supports a great story? And how do you deliver your story so people sit up and nod approvingly?

Here are eight keys to a great story:

Structure
A story (like a good book or movie) needs an opening, a set of actions, and a resolution. For a business story, think SAR (Situation, Action, Result). If your story starts and continues without structure, you'll likely lose your audience. Build your story in pieces first to create the structure, then learn to share the story so it's soft on the ears.

Enthusiasm
A story should be used to engage and to convince. If you don't seem

excited to share the story, why should anyone else want to hear it? It's not about uncharacteristic physical energy. It's about voice inflection, planned pauses, and facial expressions that show your excitement.

Honesty

A story that's made up, embellished, or even stretched will backfire. If you're unable to answer questions with detail, your story will quickly unravel. And if your interesting story can't be verified by one of your job references, that could cause a problem, too. In either case, your false tale tells a story of its own: one that leads your audience to not believe anything else you say.

Engagement

To engage people, you have to consistently maintain eye contact. If you know your stories, this shouldn't be a problem. If your story is new or not well practiced, you're more likely to shift your eyes away while searching your mind for the next key point. So practice telling your story, preferably with another person.

Details

Stories are more believable, more hard-hitting, and more interesting when key details are shared. This applies especially in the middle of your story when you talk about how what you did affected the situation. A complex situation that ends in great results is suspect without rich details to hold it together.

Length

Your social networking or elevator pitch should be 30 to 60 seconds- -perfect for quick interactions with new people. But a job interview is 30 to 60 minutes, which means your story can be longer, too. Be prepared to tell your story in three to five minutes.

Relevance

If you've asked questions in a prior job interview or earlier that same day, you'll know some of the company's key issues or opportunities. Your stories need to reflect this knowledge. You need to illustrate your experiences, characteristics, and results, telling a story that reinforces key points from your marketing materials and reflects the known needs of the company or hiring manager.

Teamwork

It's easy to create stories where you're the hero, where, despite great odds, you saved the company from imminent disaster. But one person rarely saves the day. It's usually a team, and hiring managers understand this. So be clear about your role. It's not just about honesty, it's about creating a true impression of your real skills. It also shows you're able to work well with others.

CHAPTER DISCUSSION QUESTIONS

1. What stories are you trying to tell?

2. Where are you getting stuck?

3. Who is the hero and beneficiary in each of your stories?

Target Practice

14

How To Choose Your Target Companies

"It is far more important to be able to hit the target than it is to haggle over who makes a weapon or who pulls a trigger."

Dwight D. Eisenhower

Everyone looking for a job should have a list of ten target companies. These are companies where you'd like to work if a position came open matching your skills and experience. Not having this list puts you at a distinct disadvantage when networking.

You see, I may not remember everything about you. But I am likely to remember a few of the companies you shared with me. Why? This is a very tangible bit of information.

And target companies are a key component of your job search objectives that we discussed in chapter 9.

So to answer the question about choosing target companies, you first have to identify the possibilities.

Task: Build a list of 100 companies.

Selection criteria?

1. in your industry and

2. in your target geography

Start with the ones you know. Determine whether they have an office/territory in your target geography. Get in your car and drive around key industrial areas and keep your eyes open for companies as you drive down the freeway (sounds funny, but it works). Find others in your network who are targeting the same industry and ask for their list. Use the internet, the local chamber of commerce or a local business journal.

Task: Shrink the list to 50 companies.

Selection criteria?

1. company size

2. industry sector

Do you want to work for a really big company with a powerful brand and big budgets? Or would you rather be a part of a younger, more nimble start-up?

Is there a segment of the industry that you like better? Athletic apparel vs. outdoor? Shoes vs. t-shirts?

Once complete, this new list of 50 or so will be your big target list. These are the companies you are really feeling good about and want to share with others. And you are free to share this larger list with your close-in network. But I have one more task for you.

Task: Reduce the list to 25 target companies.

Selection criteria?

1. Name Recognition

2. Cultural Fit

I say name recognition because I think that helps. If people in your network have never heard of any of these companies (especially the people not in your industry), they will be less likely to make the connection if they see a job advertised.

And culture is important. Make sure that your top 25 represent a place you'd really like to work. If you are really into casual Fridays or company picnics, find out where all that happens and put them in your top 25.

And then rotate through these 25 as you meet new people. Choose ten to share for events where the crowd will have the best opportunity to know someone at your target companies Why 10? An easy number for people to swallow and a list you can quickly communicate to people.

But what if my top 10 target companies have no jobs for me?

That's OK. Because while these are target companies, they are also examples of the types of companies where you'd like to work. Any suggestions from your network with jobs from similar companies will be welcome, right?

So now you know how to choose them.

CHAPTER DISCUSSION QUESTIONS

1   Do you have a process to choose your target companies?

2. Where can you include target companies in your marketing materials?

3. How do you penetrate your target companies?

15

How To Penetrate Your Target Companies

*"An army of principles can penetrate
where an army of soldiers cannot."*

Thomas Paine

Most job seekers meet somewhere between 3-5 people at their target companies during an interview process. And that's pretty lousy if you are interested in working for them someday. And usually those "3-5" were people they met once. On interview day.

"Not good. But what is the value of meeting more people?"

Well, obviously, the more people you meet the more knowledge you'll have. About how the target company works. And about who is pulling the switches and turning the dials. You can meet them well in advance of your first HR contact. You can research them in advance of your first interview. And, really important? You can test them out (friendly, stuffy, social) on interview day.

But there is also the awareness campaign that you should be doing with target companies. Well in advance of a more traditional approach (e.g. sending a resume).

"To make yourself known to possible interviewers or HR staffers."

And you should be actively looking to penetrate your target companies throughout the process, during an offer negotiation as well as during your first 90 days.

**The more you are known to your target company,
the better your odds of finding a job there.**

Make sense?

Just to be clear, though. To penetrate means that you create awareness of your candidacy/unique skills with as many people as possible. Once everyone knows you (or knows of you), the risk in interviewing you and hiring you goes down. Especially important in a hiring market that favors the employer.

So how do you penetrate a company in advance and during your interview process?

LinkedIn
Hopefully you know by now the value of LinkedIn and the brilliance in using your connections to reach a much broader crowd. Many may work now or in the past at your target companies. You absolutely have to be actively building a strong network here and actually using it. Find out what groups people at your target companies have joined and become a member. That way you can e-mail them directly and begin to network within the group.

Twitter
If your target companies are on Twitter, follow them. Re-tweet them. If they blog, re-tweet their blog posts with a supportive comment. Create a Twitter list of the "Top 10 Tech Co's in Atlanta". Start to send @ messages to start a conversation. And direct messages to begin a real dialogue.

Facebook

If they have a business page on Facebook (formerly a fan page), become a regular contributor there. First "like" their page and then begin providing feedback. "Share" and "Like" their content.

Charity

If you check the company website, you might find that they are involved in a few local or national charities. Consider attending local events where company personnel will be on site. Make sure that if you go, you have a good idea of how to talk to strangers (see chapter 21 to learn how to talk to strangers).

Phone/Desk Staff

Upbeat and friendly never hurts you. So every opportunity you have to network, should be taken. Even if only a brief few seconds, your demeanor matters. To someone who gets hammered all day with requests, a simple "how's your day", if it is genuine, can reach someone and help you on the day you arrive for the interview.

And don't think the opinion of the phone operator or greeter is insignificant.

Ask To Meet Others

I always asked during the interview whether I could be introduced to others. People on the team I would manage, others working at the same level or in an adjacent department. Or someone in a key cross-functional support role. All they can say is "no".

But don't just ask HR. Ask the people you interview with if there are others at the company who would be open to a few questions. Hey, you never know, maybe you'll get an invite to the company Monday Night Football party.

Company Tour

Does your target company give a tour of any of their facilities? What if you called and asked? You might meet a lot of people used to sharing a lot of information. How about a company store? Consumer relations?

Blogging/Public Relations

If you have a blog. Especially if it is industry related (technology) or key function related (marketing), you could highlight your target companies. In support of your Twitter top 10 list. Highlight key initiatives, new products or the upcoming charity event. And then send a link to their public relations team or firm.

Company Website

Who runs the website at your target company? How about writing up some feedback for the webmaster? Or writing a review of their site on your blog? Offer to write a product review on Amazon. This one is endless!

Industry Conferences

Find out where your target companies go to show off their new products and services. While you might have to drive a few hours or get on a plane, this is a target rich environment. Since other similar companies will likely be there as well.

So you can see by trying a few of the ideas above, you can become known to your target companies. In a way that should be seen as highly beneficial to both parties. Assuming your approach is a confident one. And you are not appearing desperate.

And hopefully you can see how each of these work together as part of an integrated strategy to build awareness of you and the impact you could have on their company.

CHAPTER DISCUSSION QUESTIONS

1. Who would you like to meet at a target company?

2. What affect will "more penetration" have on your confidence during a key interview?

3. Can you pick one idea from above to help you penetrate a target company?

16

Create A Target Profile
For Networking

*"You are a product of your environment.
So choose the environment that will best
develop you toward your objective. "*
W. Clement Stone

Successful job search requires many things. But primary to that is having a strong career and social networking plan.

It includes throwing a wide net to make sure those around you know that you are out of work. Sounds simple, I know. But so few of you that I meet are doing this.

So this is about career or social networking with a purpose. Because, career or social networking without a purpose is just socializing. And while we like to socialize, it's not something we should be willing to do three nights a week when we need to be creating momentum in job search.

It is hard to explain to your family when you come home with a bunch of business cards. And no real clue as to why you have them or what you'll be doing with them.

So lets start with a reminder of our very clean, specific and straightforward job search objectives

"I am looking for a director level position in apparel sales based on the West Coast. My target companies include Nike, Under Armour, Adidas."

Now you need to identify a target network profile. To identify who are your ideal career or social networking contacts. Because while throwing a wide net is smart, throwing smaller ones is even smarter.

So based on the job search objectives above, how do you create a profile that's actionable?

Here are the sections on the profile:

Industry

List your core industry (apparel) and a few others that are adjacent or complementary. Your goal is to meet people in/around your industry who may know of jobs available today or being considered for the future.

Level

Center of target is one level above you. So in this case we're looking for VP level contacts. This way you can focus important time and attention on those who would hire you or perhaps be a peer of someone who might.

Geography

Our objectives say West Coast so the profile should identify the states or cities within your geography. In this case, that would be CA, NV, OR, WA, AZ

Function

Sales is a top priority of course, but think also about other functions that work closely with or rely heavily on the function you are targeting. In this case I would include marketing and operations. Both are tied closely to the sales function and have an interest in the company bringing on smart new people around them.

Companies

You know the companies. They are your target companies. And you have to have a nice long list of them. Need help creating a list of target companies? See chapter 14.

Status

Your effort should include a plan to target fellow job seekers who fit your profile. But, more important, focus a big chunk of time on the tougher and more valuable targets. Your career and social networking effort should include targeting employed people.

And here's what the profile looks like when you are done:

Tim's Strategy 🌀 **Target Network Profile**

Industry	Apparel, Action Sports, Footwear
Level	VP
Geography	CA, OR, NV, AZ, WA
Function	Sales, Marketing, Operations
Companies	Adidas, Under Armour, Nike, Oakley
Status	Employed and Seeking

©Tim's Strategy™ www.timsstrategy.com

So now you have a plan. And a purpose to your career and social networking activity. If you choose to create a target profile, that is. And decide to focus your efforts on these people.

Not just those who walk in front of you at a networking event.

CHAPTER DISCUSSION QUESTIONS

1. Do you have a list of targeted people to meet for networking?

2. What does purposeful networking look like for you?

3. What tools can you use to get in touch with targets?

17

On Becoming A Person Of Influence

"There is nothing with which every man is so afraid as getting to know how enormously much he is capable of doing and becoming."

Soren Kierkegaard

Whether you are looking for a job, building a consulting practice or starting up a new company, becoming a person of influence can deliver great rewards – both personal and professional. Even though "who you know" still matters, it is now "who knows you" that matters most.

So, in a competitive networking environment, how do you stand out and become someone others want to know?

Here are my 10 ways to become a person of influence:

Blogging

Blogging is a great way to put yourself out there in a way that you largely control. You can write as often as you want, but be consistent. Think about where you want to influence others (what industry or function) and create a blog topic where you have passion and some ongoing ideas about content.

A great example of someone who does this well is Kevin Liebl who created a blog on leadership. He adds value to his network which is now growing every day. And you can have that too. You can read Kevin's leadership blog at kevinliebl.com.

Twitter

Some of you have joined Twitter and found it to be a great value. A fun way to network with people, learn new trends and share ideas. It is all that. It can also be a place to build your personal brand and, as a result, build influence.

The tweets you share, the links or interesting ideas you re-tweet and the conversations you have all play a role in either building influence or tearing it down.

You can also build influence through lists. Create a great one that others follow and you are now someone of value.

LinkedIn

There are many ways to build influence via LinkedIn. You can answer questions from others and you can be an active participant in your groups. Especially if you are helping others, you can become someone that others look to for advice and new ideas (= influence).

You can also start or offer to help manage a group. Group owners or moderators have just enough power to be dangerous. Used for good, you can create a group and hold the key to a valuable network. You can see an example on the Tim's Strategy Group On LinkedIn. And you are welcome to join!

Start A Movement

What do you care about? Anything at all? If not, you might want to skip this one. But if you do have an interest in the world, ask yourself: is anyone doing anything about it? You could, you know.

An extra two hours a day during your job search or in the evenings if you are working is enough to start a small movement.

Just ask Sven Johnston who lives in Orange County, CA and was tired of LinkedIn reflecting his location as "Greater Los Angeles". He started "We Are Orange County!" to create a small groundswell. Guess what, it worked. Based on Sven's effort, Orange County is now part of LinkedIn's geography breakout.

Create A Product

It can be anything, really. But ideally it is something that utilizes a natural skill of yours. It can be something that helps others, something to improve work-flow at the office or improve safety for the local elementary school. The basic act of creating is influential because so few people take the time do it. If you do it, you'll stand out. A lot of great ideas come out of necessity.

A recent one from me is a new feature on Tim's Strategy . . . The Career Expert Directory. There are now over 60 experts across 7 categories. In case you need one. And it solved a problem for me. Now when someone asks if I know a resume writer, personal branding expert or career coach, I now point them to the Career Expert Directory. All experts are pre-approved. By me.

Become A Subject Matter Expert

Neal Schaffer did this originally focused on LinkedIn. He wrote a great book on LinkedIn. He has expanded his influence into all aspects of social media. And is now building a successful social media marketing practice creating social media strategies for businesses. From relative obscurity to subject matter expert, speaker, blogger, consultant, etc in just a few years. What's in your wallet?

Be A Super Connector

You probably know a few of these people already. But you could become one too. Everyone they meet is a potential new friend. And every time they meet you, they are thinking: who can I connect (name) with?" It's not hard, it just takes time and desire. To have this kind of influence. Want an easy way?

Download the Watchlyst™ from the tools page at Tim's Strategy – a free spreadsheet to keep track of the job search objectives of those in your network.

Become A Speaker

Of course if you absolutely hate speaking (or your Toastmasters membership ran out), you can also be a trainer or a one-on-one helper. To others looking for work or learning how to network. You get speaking engagements by being good at it, having great/innovative content and being ready when the call comes.

Need a great speaker on networking for an upcoming corporate event, contact Thom Singer. An author, a powerful story teller and a great results-oriented business development leader. You can learn more about him at ThomSinger.com.

Write An E-Book

I created two of these early on. Both are free and you can download them for free on the tools page. It doesn't have to be listed on Amazon or in Barnes & Noble to get you noticed. But it has to be good and not a self-promotion or advertising piece.

Volunteer

I wrote about volunteering on the blog a while back and it got a great response. So I know this is something a lot of you do or want to do in the future. So why not now? In transition? Volunteer at your local networking group. Think about how many people will come up and talk to you once you show off that fancy and official volunteer badge. It really works. And it puts you in a position to help others.

So, here's your task for today. Pick one way to become a person of influence and get started. Unless, of course, you are already famous.

CHAPTER DISCUSSION QUESTIONS

1. What is your subject matter expertise?

2. How could you best deliver your expertise (speaking, writing, helping)?

3. What organizations need your help or expertise?

Networking With A Purpose

18

Without A Purpose It's Just Socializing

*Efforts and courage are not enough
without purpose and direction.*

John F. Kennedy

A number of months ago I shared one of my favorite presentations. With one of the best career networking resource groups in Orange County and likely one of the best in the world.

Saddleback Church is well known for its popular pastor, Rick Warren. His huge bestselling book called "The Purpose Driven Life". And their newest site called The Peace Plan.

But its career ministry might be the hidden gem. A huge group of volunteers ready to support people who really need help in this economy.

And one night in 2010, over 250 people showed up to hear me share a few ideas.

It was an amazing night. After the event, I spoke to a ton of people and learned their stories. We talked a lot about career networking. And how to be productive while doing it.

And as I was speaking with someone, these words came out:

Networking Without A Purpose Is Just Socializing

I spoke that night about having a purpose in every thing you do. And networking is no exception.

If you've been out of work for a while, you've probably come to enjoy seeing your new friends at each networking event. Sharing war stories and laughing (later, of course) about strange things that have happened along the way.

And some of that is important. To connect with your friends and networking community.

But if this is the extent of your career networking effort, you might just be spinning your wheels. Making very loose connections with a lot of nice people. When you should be working with a purpose.

And there are many more purposeful things you can target while networking. Every event you attend. Every one-on-one coffee you organize. Each should include a purpose. One that you identify on Monday morning when you plan your week.

Need help in planning?

Here's a simple tool you can use each week:

THIS WEEK [In] MY JOB SEARCH I WILL...

- No. 01 _____
- No. 02 _____
- No. 03 _____
- No. 04 _____
- No. 05 _____
- No. 06 _____
- No. 07 _____
- No. 08 _____
- No. 09 _____
- No. 10 _____

Tim's Strategy T
www.timsstrategy.com

So what are some examples of purpose-driven goals in career networking? So you can add them to your list.

1. To find a key contact at a target company

2. To secure an informational interview with an influencer in your industry

3. To help others get leads and meet key people in your circle of friends

4. To get your resume into the system of a key recruiter in the area

5. To find a career expert who can help create great marketing tools for you.

That way, you are acting with a plan. A plan that will lift you up, build your confidence and help structure the hours you spend away from the house. That way you are not acting impulsively.

And you are certainly not just socializing.

CHAPTER DISCUSSION QUESTIONS

1. Are you someone who likes to socialize?

2. How could you become more purposeful in your networking?

3. Where are you acting with impulse in your job search?

19

The 20 Successful Habits
of Networking

I never could have done what I have done
without the habits of punctuality, order, and
diligence, without the determination to
concentrate myself on one subject at a time.

Charles Dickens

This topic has become so critical for everyone, hasn't it?. Whether you are looking for work, new consulting opportunities or ways to grow your small business, career networking is absolutely essential.

But how do you do it? What are the best networkers doing and how are they doing it?

Here I've separated the 20 habits into two sections: things to be and things to do:

10 Things To Be

1. Be Memorable – Grabbing the positive attention of people at networking events is critical. And the way you do that is to have a great story. A great elevator pitch that includes something compelling. It will be different for all of us. Some are personal stories of triumph. Others are tales of work successes. But you need a story to engage people. Period.

2. Be Patient – You will meet all sorts while networking. Many of whom will not do it right. They will make mistakes. The "new", the "impatient" and the "needy" will find their way to you. And your reaction to them is critical. Instead of looking for an out, look for the opportunity to educate. You will be thanked and remembered for that...

3. Be Consistent – Don't crawl under a rock and don't expect that showing up at a quarterly event will properly freshen your career networking relationships. You need to pick a few key organizations or events and go consistently. This way you become a part of the fabric. And you start to build friendships that will now extend beyond your visits. Set a goal for yourself that gets you in one general and one industry or function specific group event per month.

4. Be Relevant – You are relevant if people attending events see you as having value. To them. Right now. How do you do that? First, keep up friendships and each time you re-connect, ask great questions to make sure you know what is happening in their lives. This allows you to offer value that is specific to them. If it is a job search driven group, offer to serve as a volunteer and create subject matter expertise. Be the resume expert for your group. Or the job interview prep person. If you help someone achieve their objectives in life, you are relevant.

5. Be Social Media Savvy – To be effective in today's world, you really need to be savvy in social media. It is the easiest and most effective way to keep in touch with your network. In a personal way. Twitter, LinkedIn, Facebook, Foursquare to name a few. If haven't already done so, get started today. Really.

6. Be Honest – In order to really do this right, you have to be honest with people. If you tell everyone what they want to hear and promise the world, the results will be poor. If someone approaches you the wrong way, I encourage you to tell them. "Hey, I appreciate what you are trying to do, but…". You can make great friends with people by helping them see the benefits of selfless networking. Those who come to an event as only a "taker" will find frustration in this new economy. Unless someone like you gently straightens them out.

7. Be Influential – How do you build influence? In short, it has to do with creating a sense in your network that you have something unique to offer. Something you've created. A group, a presentation, a helpful spreadsheet (for example). You can also do it by being selfless. Over time, your good acts will create a wave of positive momentum. And people will come to events looking for you. That makes networking easy. And fulfilling.

8. Be Considerate – If you bruise your network, it will be less pliable. Less interested in supporting you when you need it. And I think we all know that this new economy has been a teachable moment for us all. Don't ask for more than you deserve. Don't disregard a networking request if you can help it. And don't over-use a networking contact.

9. Be Thankful – Say thank you. And display your thanks in more ways than one. Know the needs and wants of your network. So that you can give targeted gratitude. Instead of something coming back to bite you, this effort will come back to kiss you. Gently on the cheek.

10. Be Present – In order to do this really well, there will be sacrifices. Less time at home with family. Less American Idol. Less Sunday football. OK with that? Being present means that you are there. At the events. And are there mentally as well. Focused uniquely on whoever is standing in front of you. It means having the ability to move around and "be present" with as many people as possible.

10 Things To Do

1. Take Selfless Action – Decide to go to an event with the sole purpose of only helping others. Not ready for full commitment? How about the first 5 people you meet? Every question from you. Your focus. Is on their needs. Not yours. Think that would feel good? It does. And it is not a waste of time. Because while a rare person will walk away having sucked you dry, most will want to make sure to ask about your needs. Regardless, it will be a nice break from your own "needs". One way to do this is to adopt someone new at the event. Someone who is clearly smart but uncomfortable. Introduce them to a few folks and then look for the next person standing on the outskirts looking for a friend.

2. Show Relational Intelligence – I wrote last year about relational intelligence for job search a while back after interviewing Steve Saccone, author of a book called "Relational Intelligence". Steve is a pastor up at Mosaic church in Los Angeles. Summing up this concept? It is "the capacity to connect with other people with skill, warmth, authenticity and compassion". If you have this capacity or show an interest in developing it, then I am in.

3. Provide Introductions – Really good career networkers are called "Super Connectors" because they have a passion for connecting people. And, over time, they meet more and more people that might be a good friend to someone they already know. You can do this at events, via e-mail, on LinkedIn and even on Twitter. For example, if you thought two guys you met should know each other, you could post this on Twitter:

"@Steve Jobs You should meet @BillGates for coffee.
Lots in common for sure!"

Whether they actually meet is up to them. But you have started the ball rolling and, as a result, may gain "influencer" status for having done so.

4. Build Real Friendships – While it is easy to go to events and build acquaintances, a great goal of career networking is to slowly develop real friendships. You can't do it with everyone of course, but when you connect with someone, don't let that moment pass. Set up a series of coffee meetings to create multiple impressions. It takes about three personal meetings to turn a first meeting into something that looks like a friendship. And it is not just the time. It's also the commitment. Demonstrated by completing a few transactions (i.e. doing something for each other). This builds mutual trust which is critical to that early friendship. Great example? Be the accountability partner for three people. Meet them on four successive Fridays and keep them on task!

5. Speak Boldly – This is a pet peeve of mine. When people speak too softly and/or without a strong voice. First, I need to hear you. Especially when addressing a group. If I can't hear every word clearly, I will likely tune you out. If your delivery is not clear or if you me-ander, my confusion will be frustrating and I won't get your message. And I may not decide to introduce myself to you after the intros are over. Finally, if your delivery is timid, I won't know that you are ready to do what you say. So be strong in your words. Let me hear you. And give me a reason (or two) that I can invest some productive time in a conversation with you.

6. Know Objectives Of Others – How do you do this? Ask really good questions. Why are they at the event? Looking for work? Consulting projects? Just here to help? Once you know this, you can be a much more active networker for them. And for the people you know that may value an introduction to them. One way I do this for job seekers is through my Watchlyst™. If I know you are looking for work, I will invite you to sign up for the Watchlyst job lead sharing tool so that I can keep a keen eye out for you. And perhaps send you a lead. You can keep your own Watchlyst by downloading my simple spreadsheet on the free tools page. It allows you to keep track of the objectives of those in your network. A powerful tool that helps you remember key needs of key people.

7. Remember The Early Days – Sit back from the computer and think about your first days walking into a networking event. The feeling of insecurity. Come on, we all felt a bit of that, right? You know no one. And, often, no one turns and, with a big smile, says: "Welcome!" You probably looked a little timid. A little unsure. And then remember that first person who introduced themselves. The first who sat with you and told you their secrets. Now that you remember all of that, go look for someone to help. Someone who needs your knowledge and experience. Someone whose path would become clearer as a result of spending time with you.

8. Stay In Touch – Of course after all this hard work at the event, you can't just let it all fall away. Relationships don't build by themselves. You need to stay in touch. Ask everyone you meet: where can I find you online? Once you know their Twitter and LinkedIn addresses, life gets easy. And fun. Here's a neat trick. And an alternative for the back of your Flashcard™ business card, add your social media addresses to the back.

9. Show Respect – While you shouldn't let too many rules inhibit your networking strategy, you need to be careful. Because you can bruise your network.

So respect:

1. the time of others – don't take more time than you deserve. Have a great 5 to 10 minute discussion at an event, then politely disengage so that they can move on. And so can you.

2. the network of others – don't overuse a name you were given or tell everyone you know about your new contact at XYZ company. Use the contact, report back to the provider and ask, if possible, if you can share it with others.

3. the personal information of others – don't share phone numbers or e-mail addresses with a big crowd. Be more purposeful than that.

10. Make Eye Contact – When talking with groups and especially when talking one-on-one, maintain eye contact. It shows respect and indicates you are actively listening. It is a subtle but critical action that says you are engaged and interested. One trick to use when speaking to groups? Engage someone's eyes long enough to fill a small water glass. Three or four seconds allows someone to feel they have been noticed. And that connection will give them a reason to listen more attentively to the rest of what you have to say.

11. Here's a Bonus… Smile - It says that you are open and friendly. I'm not saying to fake it. I'm saying that you should signal to others that you are comfortable in your shoes and willing to engage. Put up a "hard, business-like" persona and you may get fewer conversations and fewer follow-ups days later.

So there you have it. I hope each of these can be implemented easily.

Tomorrow or at your next networking event. These are critical characteristics and skills to build into your career networking strategy.

CHAPTER DISCUSSION QUESTIONS

1. What are your key things to do for successful networking?

2. What bad habits do you need to get rid of?

3. What benefit could you gain by implementing these suggestions?

20

Keep Career Networking
Fresh And Productive

Always first draw fresh breath after
outbursts of vanity and complacency.

Franz Kafka

Are you getting tired of it all?

Based on a report of reduced attendance at local networking events, burnout was suggested as a possible reason why (i.e. networking is not delivering the goods). Or people have stopped doing it effectively.

And I'm not sure how you are feeling about it.

This chapter is about how to avoid the fatigue. If that's what you are feeling.

Fatigue, whether the cause of reduced attendance or not, is real and leads to frustration. Because all this time you spend attending events needs to deliver value. Some kind of progress. If not, you might decide it's better to go back to scouring the job boards (it's not). At least that way you can drink your own coffee and relax at home.

So here are five ways to keep networking fresh and productive:

1. Find Some New Events – If you have become cozy at your favorite event, you may need a change. Or an influx of new events. If you go to meetup.com or LinkedIn, it is easy to find additional groups in your local area. And you can even look for a group in the next town over. If you can imagine yourself commuting there, shouldn't you be networking there?

2. Reinvent Yourself - It doesn't have to be a dramatic extreme makeover. But it is important to give yourself some new content. Maybe you write your elevator pitch all over again. And think of some new reasons why people should see you as memorable. Having new content will freshen you up like an Irish Spring commercial. And if you start whistling along, you will start feeling better about being away from home on a Monday night.

3. Avoid Your Friends Like The Plague — Hopefully you've made some new friends in your networking practice. Fellow job seekers who share your industry, passion for networking or coffee of choice at Starbucks. How wonderful that is. Now ditch 'em for a day. Run to the hills. Because it is likely you are spending way too much time with them. And disengaging from the process of meeting new people. New contacts will lead to other new contacts and potentially new job leads. Plus it gives you inertia.

4. Take A Productive Day Off – Taking the focus off of "you" for a day or night will fill you with good karma and good feelings. Of course, in this case, productive means taking a day off to focus on the needs of others. Selfless networking. It feels good and may add some new perspective on your own situation. You can also take a day off to do something important around the house, with your spouse or your kids.

5. Think Long Term – If you see networking as a means to a short-term end (finding a job), then the process will feel very different. You will have expectations that, if not met, will leave you feeling wasted.

Tired and unproductive. But if you see networking as a long-term business and contact building effort, you might find more joy in the process. And see that while there is short-term, practical value. That the real benefit is down the road.

CHAPTER DISCUSSION QUESTIONS

1. Is there such a thing as too much networking?

2. Have you experienced burnout while networking for a job?

3. How have you kept it fresh and productive?

21

How To Talk To Strangers

If a man can be gracious and courteous to strangers,
it shows he is a citizen of the world.

Francis Bacon

I spent an hour on the phone last year. Getting my teeth kicked in.

And I have to tell you that I stumbled a bit. Something I'm not used to doing. I was out of my element. Speaking to a radio audience that doesn't care how much time I spend working with and helping people with job search and career strategy in my free time. They just wanted answers. Rightly so.

And if you listened to my appearance on the Recruiting Animal Radio Show you may have an interesting view of my personality and strengths. Animal has a well-honed way of sweeping your feet out from under you.

But the places I stumbled were not his fault. They were mine. I was not able to answer some pretty basic questions he asked. Ones that, I think, seem pretty straight-forward. Not intentionally deceptive at all.

So now I'm here to answer the big one. In full detail. For the world to evaluate and comment.

His question to me:

How do you start, maintain and end a conversation with a stranger?

Why couldn't I answer that question with specifics? How do you talk with a stranger?

Well, I think that career networking is something I no longer do on a conscious level. I just do it. It has become second nature.

But as someone providing advice to new job seekers and other folks out there networking, it probably seemed suspect that my answer felt forced and vague. It is a great question that many struggle with heading into a career networking event. Especially if it is not a job search-focused event where many arrive with a common interest.

First Some General Ideas

* Bill Boorman (recruitingunblog.wordpress.com) shared a good idea to connect with people via a social networking site like LinkedIn and arrange a meeting at the event.

* Bring a friend with you. And if you have someone, that's great. As long as you don't use them as a crutch the whole night.

* You can contact the group owner in advance and try to arrange a meeting time. Once you meet the group owner, he/she can help you navigate the room or introduce you to others.

* Offer to volunteer for an upcoming career networking meeting. Be the sign-in person. You'll meet everyone.

* Get there early. It is much easier to find and meet new people in a less crowded room. And you can get comfortable/in a rhythm before the big crowd arrives.

* Ryon Harms (thesocialexec.com) suggests that leading with an offer to help is a great way to grab attention "and as the conversation develops the other person naturally starts to focus on how to help back".

* Finally, as I've shared before, look for other people who are obviously new (standing on the edge of the conversation) and go introduce yourself. They will be glad you did...

But here is my newly thought-out answer to this question. Written in the most basic form and in detail for beginners at career networking. But honestly, I think even the most veteran folks can use a few reminders now and again!

How To Start It

You find and connect with people when your eyes meet theirs. You make a connection with your eyes, smile and approach with confidence. And then you kick things off with a question. A starter or introductory question needs to be open ended so that the other person is given a wide berth in which to answer. To put their own spin on things. Everyone likes to give their ideas and opinions. The question also needs to be genuine.

Some specific examples if you are new to the group:

"Good morning! I'm a first-time visitor here and I'm looking to meet a few new people today. OK if I start with you?"

"Good morning. My name is Tim and this is my first meeting here. I was hoping to find someone who could tell me more about this group. Could I ask you a few questions?"

"Hi. I'm Tim. Looks like a great turnout this morning. Is this typical for the group?"

"Hey Mike, You look like you might know a few things about this group. What advice do you have for a new member?"

If you are not new to the group:

"Hi. I don't think we've met before. My name is Tim."

"Good morning. First time here? How can I help you?

If you approach a group in the middle of a conversation:

"Hi everyone. Do you mind if I squeeze in? I'm Tim."

"Hi. Room for one more?"

How To Maintain It

In order for a conversation to continue, there has to be some depth to it. Meaning that you need to learn something important about the other person or share something personal about yourself. Without it, a conversation skips the surface like a flat rock over a pond. Eventually sinking.

"What are you looking to accomplish over the next few years?

"What would you do next if you found a million dollars in a paper sack in the corner of the room with your name on it?"

"Why are you here tonight? Who are you looking to meet?"

"How can I help you?"

"What is the single biggest issue you are facing in your industry?"

"Are you like me? My weekends are swamped with kids sports!"

"I do a lot of volunteering. I'm currently building homes for Habitat. Have you ever done any volunteering?"

How To End It

There has to be an ending. And it will either happen naturally or one of the two people will have two initiate it. And I think the latter is better because ideally you are meeting more than just a few people during each event you attend. So you have to be able to move on after 5-10 minutes. In a way that does not feel abrupt or rude. So what words do you use? My suggested phrases:

"It's been great talking with you. Can you introduce me to anyone else here who might make a good connection for me?

"Thanks for answering all my questions. You've been great! Would you be open to a follow-up meeting over coffee?

"I appreciate your time. I'd love to meet a few more people tonight. Is there anything I can do for you before we move on?"

"Thanks for the time. Seems like we have a lot in common. Can I send you a LinkedIn invitation?"

Now it is your turn.

You tell me how you do it. And be as detailed as you can. Give specific phrases for each part.

CHAPTER DISCUSSION QUESTIONS

1. Are you comfortable meeting new people?

2. What is your most difficult aspect of the conversation (start, maintain, end)?

3. What are your most comfortable ways to start, maintain and end a conversation?

22

What's Memorable And Interesting About You?

*This search for what you want is like tracking something
that doesn't want to be tracked. It takes time to get
a dance right, to create something memorable.*

Fred Astaire

You may get asked this question at an upcoming networking event.

What's Memorable And Interesting About You?

Often by a group facilitator trying to give everyone some ideas of
what to say during the upcoming elevator speeches. It's good direction, of course. Because if you are not memorable you are, well,
forgotten. You move off the top of the mountain. Beaten down by
someone with a really good story, experience or unusual skill. You
may tumble to the bottom. And now you are climbing back up.
Pushing water.

And if you are no longer on top of the mountain, you are not "top-
of-mind". Top-of-mind means that you are among the first to be
considered for some action by someone else. A call for coffee, the
sending of a job lead, the introduction to an influential person in
their network.

This question is also asked by a fellow networker. Only your fellow
networker won't ask it quite so directly. In fact, the question may not

even be spoken out loud. It is simply assumed. That you will wow them in some small way to deserve attention.

That's why networking is hard for some. Especially those new to the task. Because they think that just showing up gets you points. And if you collect enough points you get awards. Enough awards and you get a prize of some kind. Not true.

So, what is memorable about you? Is there anything? Are you sure?

I'll bet if I interviewed you I could find at least two aspects. Aspects that would make people pay more attention when you are introducing yourself.

Because when you walk up to the crowd at a networking event. And you find a small circle to join and say hello. They'll all look at you. And be thinking the same thing.

"Wow me."

But a number of you might express frustration with this task. Because some people think the answer to the question is "nothing". Really?

So this is to help you think through this question with more depth. Because at a future career networking event, in a round of structured conversation, the question may be asked directly of everyone. And you'd sure like to have a great answer.

But more often, you will simply like to share something memorable when you build your elevator pitch. It could be an accomplishment that really reinforces your career. Or a skill that successful people in your field always display.

But its not just about being interesting while you are career networking. Having a few interesting points about yourself is just plain good for any conversation. At the office. At the little league game. At a cocktail party.

Having little gems to share can keep a conversation going and give people a reason to ask multiple follow-ups. It's OK that conversation revolve around you for a few minutes. Especially if they are genuine and intended to be conversational. Not entirely self-promoting.

And if you are not one who sits on a large book filled with lists of what makes you memorable, well, a few questions should help.

So I created a list of interview questions. And I hope that reading through them might help you find a little gem or two. Because sometimes the gems are there, you just can't see them. Or someone else needed to tell you it was OK to talk about it.

1. Where were you born? What is that town know for?
2. Were you born in unique circumstances (i.e. non-traditional)
3. How much did you weigh at birth?
4. What is the origin of your name?
5. Do you have a twin?
6. What is your best memory from childhood?
7. Where did you live while you were growing up?
8. Did you grow up with any people who are now famous?
9. Who was your childhood hero
10. Have you attended any memorable events (i.e. presidential inauguration)?
11. What are you passionate about?

12. Did you meet your spouse in a unique way?

13. What is the coolest place you ever visited?

14. What awards or medals did you win as a kid (sports, spelling, art, science)?

15. What have you always been known for?

16. What do friends give you grief about (math whiz, athletic, good at trivia games)

17. Did you have "big hair" in you past? Or other funny appearance story

18. What have accomplished anything big on your bucket list. What's next?

19. What is the origin or your name? Where did your family originate?

20. Are you related to anyone famous?

21. Have you ever met your childhood idol or hero?

22. Have you ever done anything really hard (run a marathon, complete a triathlon, read all the classics)

23. What can you do unusually well (artist, chef, writer, chess, crossword puzzle)

24. Do you have an engaging hobby (re-building cars, growing flowers, interior design)?

25. What is your best quality?

26. Have you ever written a novel, an ebook of poetry or a song?

27. What do you collect now or as a kid (bottle caps, baseball cards, dolls, wine)

28. Have your kids done anything remarkable or especially cute?

29. Have you had to overcome a challenge in your life?

30. What famous person, dead or alive, would you like to meet?

31. What one work accomplishment will you be remembered for?

And once you find two or three gems. Build a short and a long version of the story so that you can tell it. Quickly if you need to, of course. But even better? Create a long version for when you have the time. And when a conversation seems ready for it.

Career networking is not about bragging. It is about unfurling your robe to show a few bright colors to the people around you. Who, prior to that, were just seeing another normal person.

And I'll bet you are not that normal. Once you've thought about it.

CHAPTER DISCUSSION QUESTIONS

1. What's memorable about you?

2. What can you do to stay on the radar of key people?

3. What's the value of being "top-of-mind" with your network?

Confidence Is King

23

Marketing Yourself
With Confidence

*We gain strength, and courage, and confidence by each
experience in which we really stop to look fear in the face...
we must do that which we think we cannot.*

Eleanor Roosevelt

I presented a webinar to a fantastic networking group I belong to called MENG (Marketing Executives Networking Group). If you are a marketing exec, it is a significant resource both in terms of the website content and, especially, the direct access you get to some of the smartest marketers in the world.

In that webinar, I introduced a new idea. Which is a new way of talking about a concept that has been around in some form. But I wanted to focus its light on the job search and career space. To see how it looked once exposed.

Here is the basic definition:

> **Confidence marketing is the targeted and purposeful sharing of your unique strengths with the job search community**

And here's how I break it down:

"CONFIDENCE MARKETING"

The word "confidence" in this context is interesting because my head keeps thinking of the shortened version of this word or "Con". And when you combine it with "Marketing", I keep thinking "Con Man". But I really like the idea of marketing yourself with confidence. Because no one else can market you as effectively as "you". Others may be more credible (the power of a third party recommendation) but no one can sell you better. If you know who you are.

"TARGETED"

While I talk a lot about the importance of breadth in job search networking (throwing a wide enough net to make sure that everyone who should know about your search actually does know what's happening). But it doesn't mean that you should continue to talk with everyone. Because some people in your network are more valuable than others. Yes! In fact, you should be tracking and ranking your network to know not only who is the most influential but also who is most active (most open) in offering ideas, connections and leads. So target your marketing efforts accordingly. As we discussed in chapter 16.

"PURPOSEFUL"

A cousin to "targeted", purposeful is about what you do with each networking contact. Not on impulse, but rather based on a plan of action set in motion a week or a month before. Setting goals for yourself will prevent your being overly reactive to random opportunities. When I first started my blog, it was based on an analogy of plate spinning. Which is an act of efficiency. Only spinning the plates when necessary. The purpose being to keep the focus where it is needed. As I built out the analogy, I found it is more about the value of the plate (what it can do for you) less than merely spinning the ones that are slowing down.

"UNIQUE STRENGTHS"

How do you stand out in a pile of 1,000 resumes? How do you get remembered after a networking event attended by 100+ people? How do you stay on the radar of top recruiters? The answer to all? You must clearly identify who you are, what you've accomplished and demonstrate relevance to the audience. And this can be a different answer depending on the scenarios above. In the end, if you look like everybody else, you will not be remembered. It's just too hard for all of us to categorize our fast growing networks without each individual doing their part. So how do you express yourself uniquely? How do you stand out in a positive way?

"COMMUNITY"

Yes, this is a community. And it remains one after you arrive at your next great role. And in the community there are rules – both formal and informal – about how you should act. To be seen as a positive contributor. And to be remembered for the right things. In order to be a positive contributor, there needs to be a selfless aspect to your search and to your networking. If you think you are in this community to steal from it. To grab what you need and run once you arrive in your new job. That would be a bad way to go.

A line between power and humility	Acting with a purpose each and every day	Being "the pursued"

"POWER AND HUMILITY"

There is a line here that says you have to be confident, proud of your accomplishments and able to shout them out on your resume and in your elevator pitch. I am not asking you to hold back. But the way you deliver it matters. With a smile helps. And with the right amount of bravado to fit the situation.

"BEING THE PURSUED"

While you cannot always create a scenario in which you are the pursued, you can avoid appearing desperate. Notice I didn't say "feeling desperate". I think we all have faced that feeling when that job that feels so right is not offered to you. And you feel a need to pursue that company, recruiter or hiring manager. It's OK to feel it, just don't act on it. And don't allow it to come across in conversations. Because it makes you look less "in demand".

CHAPTER DISCUSSION QUESTIONS

1. Are you confident in yourself? Why or why not?

2. What makes you unique?

3. How can you change to a "be pursued" mind-set?

24

Your Personal Brand Needs You

Know yourself. Don't accept your dog's admiration as
conclusive evidence that you are wonderful.

Ann Landers

Who are you? Really. How would you like to be perceived? And which of these personas ends up speaking on your behalf to recruiters, hiring managers and fellow networkers?

Knowing who you are, where your natural talents truly fall and how to get those ideas across quickly are key to establishing and building a personal brand.

So here are three questions to ask yourself:

Who Are You?	**What Makes You Special?**	**Ready to Share?**
• Strategic • Tactical	• Philosophy • Method	• Positioning • Summary

Who Are You, Anyway?

Based on answers from people in networking rooms, I sometimes wonder just how well we know ourselves. And despite having an unusually large amount of time to think this one through, most job seekers know little about themselves and what they are really looking for in their career. But they know where they've been.

So how do you build a personal brand without a pretty good sense of who you are? And how do you get someone to pick up your flag and run with it? Especially if the flag appears to be white and without a unique design?

When you answer a question, are you expressing your real self or the self that sounds presentable to a bunch of strangers (i.e. makes you sound extra-interesting, more business-like)? If your Mom was in the crowd or your best friend from college, would they be scowling at you or smiling and nodding their head as you share the pieces of you that truly set your brand apart from the rest?

What Are Your Natural Talents?

Certain things come easy to some people. And those same things can be next to impossible for someone else. Why is that? Well beyond the "strengths and weaknesses" conversation, this asks you to not only know what you are naturally good at doing. It also asks what you enjoy doing. Very different. For example, I am strong with a budget and a P&L but give me a choice between that and a brainstorming session or a strategy discussion, I'll slide the budget over to someone else. I know that about myself.

Knowing where your true talents fall and recognizing how to capitalize on them, can make all the difference in an interview. And sometimes, being true to yourself means telling a hiring manager some real specific truths. Truths that may derail a job opportunity that you thought you really wanted. These are the same truths, however, that will line you up perfectly for the right job a few weeks later.

How Do These Get Communicated?

Are you ready to share with others? Do you have a strong elevator pitch, a clear positioning statement and a way to share these that makes others more open to receive your content? If you are standing up in front of 25 or 50 people sharing aspects of your personal brand, will anyone really care? Immediately? How about 15 minutes later after 15 others have spoken? Your authentic delivery of relevant and interesting content about YOU is necessary. That delivery will be remembered long after those that come across as vague and irrelevant. Long-winded and otherwise not meaningful loses out every time.

Your smile, your stories and your eye contact communicate character. And character makes me want to remember you.

Long after we've met.

CHAPTER DISCUSSION QUESTIONS

1. What are your natural talents?

2. What can you accomplish with these talents?

3. How do these get communicated?

25

The Tools That Enable Confidence

With realization of one's own potential and self-confidence
in one's ability, one can build a better world.

Dalai Lama

Maybe you and I are different. But I feel more confident when I have good content. And good methods to share that content. So that means you have good things to say and a compelling way to deliver the message.

In job search, your content is your history, experience and skills. Your methods include a resume, LinkedIn profile and your profiles on other social media platforms such as Facebook and Twitter.

That sounds pretty simple. And your content is illustrated by your personal brand. So this is about the tools or methods you use to highlight your personal brand. And by doing it well, providing you with materials that elicit confidence.

So now I'll introduce you to four key tools created to help illuminate your personal brand. Some of which I have referred to in the prior chapters.

There are four tools that can help here:

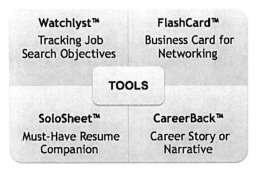

Watchlyst™ Tracking Job Search Objectives	**FlashCard™** Business Card for Networking
TOOLS	
SoloSheet™ Must-Have Resume Companion	**CareerBack™** Career Story or Narrative

Watchlyst™ • Job Share Assistant

You've probably guessed that the #1 networking tool during hard times is helping friends, family, former co-workers and other worthy folks find their next job. Whether you are employed or working at the time, it simply does not matter. But how? Use the Watchlyst to organize (on one page) the specific job objectives of those in your network. When you see a match, pass it along!

SoloSheet™ • Resume Companion

A one-sheet template (networking bio) that gets all of your critical information onto one, easy-to-digest page. It includes data that will help your network help you – something a resume does not accomplish.

CareerBack™ • Career Backgrounder and Narrative

Write your history and create a longer-term personal brand position for yourself. Your CareerBack is written in the third person (as if you are a news reporter writing an article about yourself). This way, you can do a proper job of highlighting your best points, skills and accomplishments (often hard to do properly in a resume). Most people don't feel comfortable bragging on themselves. How about you?

FlashCard™ • Business Card for Networking

Instead of a business card, I call it a FlashCard™. Why a FlashCard, you ask? Well, simply, it allows people to remember you and, this is crucial, your specific job objectives... in a flash.

For these and more tools, go to timsstrategy.com and click on the "tools" page.

CHAPTER DISCUSSION QUESTIONS

1. What tools are you using to build confidence?

2. How do you create your message in a compelling way?

3. How skilled are you at delivering that message?

26

17 Ways To Build Confidence

Believe in yourself! Have faith in your abilities!
Without a humble but reasonable confidence in your
own powers you cannot be successful or happy.
Norman Vincent Peale

The process of finding a job can suck the life out of you. It can drain your best parts. When you need them most. Here are ways to build your confidence.

Of course to embark on the "getting them back" journey, you have to realize that you've lost them in the first place.

That's the first hurdle. Because losing confidence doesn't happen all in one day. And it doesn't get reported on a computer screen as if you were playing a video game.

There's no "confidence bar" that tells you when you've lost 25 or 50 percent of your strength after a piece of bad news or a bad interaction with someone in your network.

Good thing too as the knowledge of any loss could put you in an immediate tail-spin. Since "confidence lost" becomes worry and concern. And sometimes panic.

Below I will share or reinforce 17 ways to re-fill your tank. Build your confidence. Bonus points, if you will. Ready?

1. Set weekly goals for yourself. And achieve the bulk of them.

Proving to yourself each week that you are getting somewhere reinforces your confidence.

2. Add new people to your network. Career networking should never be static. It must be dynamic – constantly changing. New people equal new life and new extended networks. And inevitably, new leads.

3. Take a day off and help others. Doing so will breath new life into your effort. And the help that you give others that day will come back and smile upon you.

4. Pay attention to your small wins. Join my LinkedIn group and participate in a great discussion there. About how paying attention to small wins can nudge up your self-belief.

5. Re-write your elevator pitch. Add a new wrinkle that allows you to be better remembered. Add a shorter or longer version that allows you to be ready for any situation. Instead of trying to cram 90 seconds of "you" into 30.

6. Write specific and tangible job search objectives. Make sure you find ways to get your new objectives communicated to your growing network. As well as all the people who are already looking out for you.

7. Write a regular e-mail update to your network. Whether it is weekly or monthly, be consistent. By reminding everyone of your continued candidacy, you keep them engaged and in your corner. So few people do this. And if you do, you will stand out.

8. Remember your past victories. In addition to paying attention to victories within job search, also remember prior days when you were at your best. We all had big days that defined us early on in our careers. Go back and read your performance reviews or scan the awards on the wall of your home office. You were great at least once or twice. And will be great again soon.

9. Find a career expert. Someone who can help guide you through this big challenge in life. A career coach, resume writer or personal branding expert can help a great deal. Whether you need a kick in the rear or a shoulder to lean on.

10. Start (or join an existing) accountability group. Meet on Fridays to keep everyone in the group focused. Focused on achieving their goals. To avoid procrastination – the enemy of a successful job search. And to keep your momentum strong.

11. Add some new skills. Take a class in a related field. Or take an advanced seminar. Something you can talk about in your next interview. Or draw from as you explain your strengths to a recruiter or HR person.

12. Go do something good in the world. A few hours a week. Volunteering during job search can be a confidence builder. As you meet new people and build your influence in the community.

13. Learn how to talk with strangers. If you get really good at conversing with new people. You will naturally feel more comfortable each new time you come in contact with strangers.

14. Have a purpose in everything you do while finding a job. Avoid impulsive behavior. And make you are networking with a purpose. And paying attention to those who can help you the most.

15. Know thyself. Establish and live your own personal brand. Follow bloggers like Dan Schawbel, Ryan Rancatore, Thom Singer,

Meg Guiseppi, Neal Schaffer who can help you define your message. And put yourself in situations where you know you can succeed.

16. Be totally ready to interview. Throw out your old ways and get yourself completely prepared. Use smart interview prep tools and enjoy the knowledge that you have done everything you can to knock 'em dead.

17. Re-write your networking bio and create some new networking business cards. New personal marketing materials can boost you up like few other things. Because you can touch them. And give them to others. They make you feel a bit new again. Like a fancy new suit or pair of new shoes.

CHAPTER DISCUSSION QUESTIONS

1. Are you setting weekly and monthly goals for your job search?

2. How are you preparing for important meetings and interviews?

3. Who is helping you stay accountable to your goals?

Preparing For A Big Interview Day

27

Smart Interview Preparation (Sip™)

Hibernation is a covert preparation
for a more overt action.

Ralph Ellison

If you've been to my site before and think I am heading over the deep end with all the tools, you'd be partly right. The problem is that the feedback has been pretty good. So you'll just have to put up with a few more. And maybe a few more after that...

The Sip™ tool is designed to walk you through a structured process to prepare for a strong and focused interview. Strong preparation supports a confident and direct conversation about your real skills and your ability to immediately impact the interview team.

While it is thorough in some ways, it is not intended to cover every possible angle. Because you can kill yourself preparing for unlikely questions.

What I like about these tools is the structured process they force you through. Especially during job search — where it is easy to get subjective/emotional – your ability to remain focused and smart will help you in so many ways. How?

Simple example:

It's been eight weeks since you were laid off and you've had no interviews. You finally get a phone interview and, surprise, you are offered a first round in-person interview at a target company.

Great news all the way around, right? So where's the issue?

The issue is that the eight week wait likely has you hyper-focused on this new job opportunity. Mostly a good thing. But the risk is that your focus puts too much pressure on the upcoming day.

You cram as much thinking as possible into your preparation and, as a result, ignore all other potential opportunities. You stop networking and perhaps are slow to call back recruiters or HR managers. Why would you, right? A great job is just a few days away!

Here are a few risks of a hyper focus on one opportunity:

1. As stated above, your focus on the upcoming interview leaves you unfocused on other opportunities. And, in my experience, opportunities come in waves of twos and threes.

2. Pushing hard on two or three opportunities provides perspective and takes some pressure off each individual interview. Less pressure means you can be your confident self, realizing that all is not riding on this one day.

3. If you don't get an immediate call back or you don't eventually get an offer, it can put you in a sour mood for weeks. If it was not meant to be, you need to be able to let it go. Easier to do when other calls or meetings are already scheduled for next week.

So, what does a smart interview preparation process look like? Oh, and how can I get one?

Well, to me, it breaks down like this:

Company Name. Interview Date. Location and Start Time.

Whether you have two weeks or two days to prepare, it is important to start with the basics. Map the location and drive it a day or two before the interview. Drive it at the same time you'll be driving a day or two later. Arrive early. This helps you relax.

Company History and Culture.

You can learn a great deal from a look at where a company has been. Have there been struggles (financial or strategic)? Is it a new product rich environment or a company relying upon historical products or services to succeed today. What do these things say about the culture? Importance of innovation? This may be an important component for you as you identify a target company.

Industry Trends and Competitive Review

What's happening in the company's industry may have an impact on its decision making. Are there any large macro issues facing them and their competitors? For example, are they uniquely impacted by high gas prices? Who are their competitors and what are their new products. Does the company have number one brands or is it a second tier company in a very competitive category?

Now, before I go any further, you might be saying to yourself: "But I'm looking for an IT job! Why do I need to know all of this?" It may be that you don't need to know all this information, but depending on who you meet, a knowledge of the company and its culture cannot hurt you!

Company Strategy and Recent Results

What is the stated objective of the company? Where is it looking to go? If you are in IT, what might the impact be on the company's use of technology? Is the company riding a few big recent successes? Or has it struggled to get traction.

Interview Team Vetting

Who will interview you? Can you find out in advance? If so, look them up on Google or Linkedin. How long have they worked for the company? Have they spent their entire career in this industry? If the hiring manager has been in his/her position for less than a year, they will be more likely to listen to messages of change than if they've been in that role for 10 years. A more established manager might be more defensive to a more aggressive approach. This knowledge also helps in developing a person-specific list of questions.

Key Product Review And Usage Results

Whether the company makes widgets, rents cars, makes music videos or builds condos, find a way to get some personal experience with their product or service. For example, prior to my interview with a company that makes car wax in 2005, guess what I did? I washed and waxed my car. Twice.

Really? Absolutely.

And it made a huge difference in the interview. I was able to give them personal feedback on my experience with their products and it showed an early engagement and interest in their products.

The other value? My car was sparkling on interview day – something they look for in candidates.

So, ask yourself, how can you show a similar interest in the products or services of your target company? Of course, if you work in certain industries (Bio Tech or Pharmaceuticals) you may have to be careful!

Specific Job Requirements vs. My Strengths and Experiences

As simple as it sounds, list out the requirements and how you line up against them. Part of your job in this first interview is to prove (through a deeper look and via specific examples) your excellent fit with the job description the company worked so hard to create. Know where you are especially strong and where you may have to try a bit harder.

Identify Three Relevant and Measurable Successful Experiences

Be prepared to tell a great set of stories about how you've had a significant impact on other companies. And be able to relate them back to the challenges or opportunities described by the hiring company. Be ready to describe in a compelling way how these experiences make you uniquely qualified to step into this new role and succeed. Tomorrow.

Questions? Beginning. Middle. End.

Be prepared to show a genuine interest in the ways of the company, the hiring manager, the current challenges, the team, etc. And make sure you have questions prepared for each part of the interview. Early on, try a question that establishes a more conversational tone to the interview vs. a traditional Q&A format. Questions in the middle should show your depth of thinking and allow you to learn key details to help you cement fit with the position. Questions at the end should show your interest in the company's future and perhaps the role that the department might play.

Positioning Objective

How would you like to be remembered by each interviewer? In addition to your being a great fit with the job description and, hopefully, a good fit culturally and personally, what will make you the ideal candidate? What will be the one thing that makes an interviewer gush over you in the post-interview wrap-up? You are in the car heading home. They are talking about you. What do you want them saying? Was it your energy? Your breakthrough ideas? Your work ethic?

Post Interview Reactions

So you survived. Now before you turn on the AC and pull out on down the road, take a few minutes to jot down your initial reactions. What does your gut say? Bubbling with excitement or really unsure? You need to react to the people but you also need to react to the messages and the energy of the office environment. For example, if you are a people person and no one smiled at you during your walk-through, what might that tell you?

There. That's my Sip™.

You can download a form for this tool on timsstrategy.com.

I hope it helps you prepare for your next interview. Even more, I hope it helps you focus and feel smart as you step into the office of your first interviewer.

Oh, and I hope you knock their socks off.

CHAPTER DISCUSSION QUESTIONS

1. What does your current interview preparation process include?

2. How could a mock interview help solidify your positioning?

3. What questions can you ask during the interview to help you decide fit?

28

Heard But Not Seen:
The Phone Interview

I want to live every moment totally and intensely.
Even when I'm giving an interview or talking to people,
that's all that I'm thinking about.

Omar Sharif

Phone interviews have largely replaced the first interview for a lot of companies and are often completed by someone in HR – not the hiring manager – to act as a screener for first round interviews. They are often asking questions to both weed you out and to figure out your fit for the job.

Some quick tips for the phone interview:

1. Try to schedule an early AM slot – you are fresher and they are less likely to be rushed or delayed by the slew of other duties they will face later in the day.

2. Find a private place – this limits the distractions or noises on your end and allows you some privacy to prepare, hold the interview and privately wind down or take notes on your impressions.

3. Stand up and walk around as you talk – funny how this works but you tend to sound more authoritative and strong when you are doing something vs. sitting at a desk or on a couch playing with a button on a seat cushion.

4. Make notes in advance of the call – these are your key talking points as well as the important topics that will likely come up with this employer. Phone interviews are like open book tests in school. Your ability to hit on all the right messages increases greatly if you can have a road map.

5. Smile as you talk – another funny one but it really works. It relaxes you and gives your voice a more confident and conversational sound. It may also help to create the right impression with the caller – remember you are one of 5-10 people getting a call that day.

CHAPTER DISCUSSION QUESTIONS

1   What makes a phone interview different from an in-person interview?

2. What are your objectives for this short call?

3. What personality will you convey to the caller? Is that right?

29

Surviving A Web Cam Interview

*When I talk to the camera, mate, it's not like I'm talking
to the camera, I'm talking to you because I want to whip
you around and plunk you right there with me.*

Steve Irwin

Have you ever been asked to perform in front of a camera? How about a web camera?

And how about when you are looking for a new job?

I got a question from an old friend I worked with back in the late 80's that prompted those above…

> Hi Tim,
>
> Searched the site but could not find any guideline / direction on Web Cam interviews (Mine upcoming is with the HR Manager)… If it is a topic you have discussed in the past… can you advise where it might be posted… if not… possible a discussion point down the road. Thanks… Mark

I hadn't written about this in the past, but I think web cam interviews are going to become a lot more common. Especially as the technology gets better and hiring companies get more comfortable using it.

So what should you do to survive and succeed in a web cam interview?

Get comfortable with the technology

If you don't own a web camera, go buy one. At least a week before your interview. And then do web calls with everyone you know. Buy two and send one to your parents. Your comfort level will contribute to your confidence level. On interview day, don't be surprised if an issue or two comes up (can't hear, can't see, a few second delay). These can happen and usually get worked out in the first few minutes. A lot of companies will offer you a test call to make sure it all works.

Set up a mock interview

It's one thing to talk to your Mom about the kid's weekend soccer games. It's another to talk to an HR person you don't know who lives on the opposite coast about your biggest challenge. So set up a mock interview with a friend or former boss so that you can get used to giving your pitch while staring at your computer.

Clear the room

Simply said, make sure you know what the camera sees. Ask your mock interviewer to tell you what they see. Set up your computer in a clean, well-lit room without your beer bottle or antique doll collection on the back wall. Bookshelves and fireplaces tend to be pretty good. Can be your home office if you have one. Also, make sure your room-mate, spouse and/or 6 kids are cleared out (30 minutes before and after your scheduled call). A fight over the new video game won't sound good in the background.

Determine a proper distance

To avoid the fishbowl effect during the interview, make sure you ask your friends/mock interviewer how you look. For me, I'd like to see you from the waist up. A little tighter is OK, but much more and you are "all face". Some programs will allow you to see how you look from the start allowing you to adjust on the fly.

Know the strength of your voice

So, I'll just say it. You don't need to yell. With most programs, your computer's speakers will work just fine. If you are one of those loud talkers on a normal conference call, don't be that person during your web cam interview. Start in your normal voice and ask nicely, "how do I sound?" and you can adjust from there.

Be professional, not stiff

Part of your task in a prelim interview is to provide detail on your qualifications for the job. But you also have an opportunity to establish a rapport with the interviewer. Some interviewers are all business, but there are many styles of interviewers. So your ability to judge their style early on will help you to succeed as the interview progresses.

Dress to impress, not to kill

You will each make your own decision on this one. It may depend on your own beliefs. Or the industry or culture you're in. But I'm going to suggest that you interview business casual via web cam. Still professional but comfortable enough that you don't look over-dressed in your own house. I'll be curious to get your reaction this suggestion. Feels right to me. And it is what I've done in the past.

Prepare like it's interview day

Make sure you treat this web cam interview like you would an in-person interview. The more you know the better, right?

Smile

You hear me say this a lot. To me, it is one of the key networking habits you need to have and something that people like to see during interviews. It says you are confident and comfortable. And excited to be talking to this company. Too much and you are going to look silly so don't over-do it. Part of the "don't be stiff" advice above.

Relax

A web cam interview is often the first in what will be a string of interview opportunities with a company. If you don't succeed, you haven't invested a lot. Nor have they. And you may find that this first interview unlocks the key to your next role. Or it may uncover a dud. Try to enjoy the process of learning about a new company and of sharing your accomplishments with others.

CHAPTER DISCUSSION QUESTIONS

1. What experience do you have on a web cam?

2. What is your biggest fear about being in front of a camera?

3. What aspects of your personality will be emphasized via camera?

30

The Tao Of Informational Interviews

The journey of a thousand miles begins with one step.

Lao Tzu

I wrote once that an elite class of employed folks wasn't doing its solemn duty. The duty? To play a proactive and positive role to support the effort of job seekers.

"Have you been a member of the employed elite?"

I received a very important reminder from a networking friend. While I included a warning for job seekers (i.e. respect your network, say thank you, and don't ask for too much), he reminded me of the pink elephant in the networking room.

That elephant is the fact that too many job seekers break the social contract of networking. They have effectively pushed some very influential employed executives out of the game. Those executives are no longer helping job seekers because their experience is that job seekers take advantage.

Specifically, he said, job seekers are blowing it during informational interviews. The classic "bait and switch".

The big "no-no"? Asking for or about a job during the informational interview.

Now, some of you in transition may say: "Are you kidding me? I go through all the trouble to do this, and I can't even ask about a job? Sounds like a long run for a short slide!"

If that's in your head, then you need to go to networking reform school. I personally think that most job seekers that make this mistake, however, do so out of ignorance or desperation. But it doesn't matter why you did it. You did it.

And as soon as you do, the original value of networking goes out the window. Instead of leaving an executive with a positive impression of you, you've put them on the defensive. Reminding them of why they normally avoid information interviews.

You see information interviews are somewhat counter-intuitive to a job seeker. It's not about immediate value (although that can be the result). It's first about learning. And about leaving a good impression.

And you can't leave a good impression if you put any pressure on this person who has kindly given up 30 minutes of their day for you. Sorry.

So, what are the benefits of informational interviews anyway?

Well, I think there are three:

1. You learn vital information about a company, industry or management team. This is the primary value that should be understood by both parties. It can help you determine whether or not your experience/skills are a good match. You may actually find that the best result of an informational interview is that you don't think there's a match. Good to know.

2. By doing the above well, you leave a positive impression with a key and potentially influential person in your target company or industry.

3. You may learn of others with whom you can have a similar discussion. On some occasions, you may even get a few job leads.

Notice that I didn't include "get a job"? That's because informational interviews are one of the building blocks of a strong job search networking effort. So you have to have a lot of patience here.

Are you a patient person?

If not, you will lose out on the great potential value. If impatient and desperate for quick results, you will push away the very person who might help you.

So, I'll use myself as an example. Here's my career bio:

Industry Expertise:
Consumer Packaged Goods, Automotive Accessories, Computer Accessories

Function:
Marketing (Product and Brand Management)

Level:
Vice President

Geography:
Southern California (primarily Orange County)

Company History:
Nestle, Tree Top, Kensington Technology Group, Mauna Loa Macadamias, Meguiar's Car Wax, Horizon Food Group

So, here are the 5 keys to successful information interviews. If you'd like to talk to me about any of the previous…

1. COMMUNICATE WELL - Send me a nice note on Linkedin or regular e-mail. In the note, tell me how you found me (referral, Linkedin, etc). Introduce yourself (and don't start with "I'm in transition"). Tell me what your objectives are in wanting to talk. Have someone else read the note to see if the tone is right. I prefer positive and thankful vs. desperate and demanding. Suggest a few times that will work for you (so I can choose one) and offer to meet me anywhere (my office is often good/easy or a local Starbucks). Be clear about how much time you need (30 minutes feels right to me).

2. MIND YOUR P's and Q's - Be on time and dress appropriately. I don't personally need you in business dress, but it should either match my dress or at least be a nice business casual. Some may expect you in a suit. Have a resume, but don't give it to me unless I ask for it.

3. STICK TO YOUR OBJECTIVES - Re-read your note to me before you arrive and stick to those objectives unless I open up other avenues with you. This is about that risk I mentioned earlier. If you pull a "bait and switch", I will not feel good about you. My mind-set will change very quickly and, even more important, my interest in helping you will diminish.

4. DON'T ASK FOR A JOB - Do not, under any circumstances, ask for a job or inquire about possible positions opening in the near future. This is the second risk and is truly the nuclear option. Because it can destroy the good faith partnership we started. But no fear. You know why? I already know that you are looking for a job. So if you follow these guidelines and leave me feeling "appropriately utilized", I will want to help you find one. It is OK to ask (at the end) if there is anyone else that I think you may benefit from meeting. Again, assuming that you will follow these same rules. If you do it right with me then lose your scruples with my network, I will pay the price. And so will you. If you do meet with a friend of mine based on my recommendation, follow up with me and let me know how it went. That may prompt a communication about you with my network. Buzz is good!

5. SAY THANK YOU - Say a hearty "thank you" and follow up with one (written is nice but an e-mail is OK too). After our introduction, I would also be open to your asking to connect on Linkedin. You can also ask: "how can I help you?"

So, what can you expect after our meeting? Well, maybe nothing. If you are disappointed then you still don't get it.

But more than likely, I will think of someone for you to call. I may send you a list of networking groups in your industry. I may tell a recruiter about you (assuming you fit a search).

Think about all of this as learning something important about an industry or company, meeting someone new and, yes, creating some good karma in the work world.

Good things come to those who wait.

Those who push their personal agenda in networking end up, well, waiting. And wondering what happened.

CHAPTER DISCUSSION QUESTIONS

1. Can you be patient enough to see the rewards of an informational interview?

2. What information are you looking for?

3. How can you use this information to help you find a job?

31

How To Signal Strength

Good actions give strength to ourselves
and inspire good actions in others.

Plato

Interviewers want you strong and confident. Not weak and desperate. This is part of the "fit" question. So how do you operate during an interview to send a message that supports your strong qualifications?

Here are ten ways to signal strength:

1. **A great handshake.** Have one?

2. **A strategic "I don't know".** Strategic doesn't mean that you make it up. Or pick a place for it randomly. It means that on a question that you may have answered as best you can in the past, instead say "I don't know" (IDK). Those words can be powerful. An honest expression and perhaps a starting point for conversation. Instead of you pretending that you know it all.

3. **A pause before you answer.** Sometimes everything is not on the tip of your tongue. And sometimes you aren't able to anticipate every question in advance. So pause and think about it.

4. **Grab a chair.** Without being too pushy, find the obvious or most obvious chair and grab a seat. Don't ask if it is OK. Or hesitate. Just grab a seat.

5. **Stay still.** While there is room for some movement, I'd rather you stay still in your chair. Excessive shifting or leg crossing does not signal strength. It signals "I'm not comfortable". Stillness suggests focus and resilience. Strength. Especially during a long interview day.

6. **Smile.** It says you are relaxed. And enjoying your interview day. Not everyone smiles. Many grimace. But that's not a smile now is it?

7. **Ask great questions.** Early on to create a conversation, in the middle to keep it going and at the end to make sure your knowledge of the company matches their understanding of you.

8. **Use first names.** Now for some of you, this is your normal way of interviewing. For others, you wouldn't think of it. After all, it would be rude to use someone's first name, wouldn't it? Really? First name = equality. There are some exceptions to this, of course. But generally, it works.

9. **Say hello.** To others you meet in the hallway, in the restroom and in the cafeteria. It's OK. You are not an experiment. You are a potential new employee there. And you might even learn a little about the company's culture based on the reaction you get.

10. **Have great stories.** And specific examples. A lot of people deliver vague answers. The smart ones have a whole treasure chest of stories. Examples of big wins, tough challenges and an occasional failure they learned from. Specifics are really important. I don't like to ask a question three times.

CHAPTER DISCUSSION QUESTIONS

1. What else can you do to signal strength in a job interview?

2. When meeting with a recruiter?

3. What actions signal weakness and how can you avoid them?

32

The Importance Of Being Yourself

*The best way to find yourself is to
lose yourself in the service of others.*
                                    Mohandas Gandhi

When I was a kid I used to play air guitar with the best of 'em. The band of choice was, of course, KISS. We'd stand on the fireplace using the various tools to stoke or clean the fireplace as our lead guitar. The music came like a landslide of rocks and debris from the loft up above.

Anyway, besides the great music, KISS was known for costumes, explosions and great makeup that hid their faces (hiding their true identity).

Do you ever interview like KISS?

What if I told you that sometimes people interview in a way that hides their identity? Their authentic self is in there, but so is the person that can better answer the interview questions being asked by the hiring manager. For example, if someone asks you if you are more comfortable being independent or getting regular direction, what do you say? Are you always looking for the middle ground so that you can be seen positively?

Have you ever answered in a way that is mostly untrue but seems to be what the hiring manager wants? Many people make errors in judgment especially if they are in round 2 or 3 and want to look like the right candidate.

Don't do it. Be your brutally honest and authentic self.

Why?

1. It's the right thing to do.
2. You will get hired at the right time for the right job by a company that wants YOU (not someone that you will struggle to live up to).
3. You will succeed long term by working at companies where you fit and can grow.

If you are not authentic, you will get jobs and then lose them (creating a trail of short, unsatisfying results).

So, don't be like KISS when out looking for a job. It's not about rocking and rolling all night. It's a career you want to be thinking about...

CHAPTER DISCUSSION QUESTIONS

1. What characteristics of a job best fit your personality?

2. Describe your ideal boss – what does he/she do or say to you?

3. How can you interview with authenticity and truly deliver "you"?

33

Interview Styles To Avoid

I generally avoid temptation unless I can't resist it.
                                              Mae West

I don't interview as many people in my current job as I used to earlier in my career. But I have interviewed enough of you to see a few interview styles pop up more than a few times. And I have to tell you that I've been scared.

Scared to the point that my blood runs cold.

Like I've seen a ghost. And felt the shiver of a thousand ice cubes running down the center of my spine.

Yes, I am talking about you. I've met you.

The truth is that you have to interview a lot of people. Kiss a lot of frogs. Before you find someone that is qualified, at the right point in their career and a good fit for the job. But for someone to deliver on those three, they need to have an interview style that allows the hiring company to visualize them in the job. Hanging out with them. And making great things happen. That's why interview styles are so important.

So I feel compelled after scouring my own hiring memory. To share with you the interview styles to avoid. And if this is you, I'm sorry. But it's time to change. Lest my blood run cold yet again.

1. Smug – Hard to imagine that smug can be found in even the toughest economy but he/she can. It is either seen when someone believes they are overly or uniquely qualified for a job, is trading down in company size or has just left an important company. In the last case, they hold on to the perceived stature they once had and projects it onto their new potential boss. Not good.

2. Perky – If you are too "up" and the interviewer is not, one of two things will happen. Either you will make them feel "up" or you will make them wonder why you are so "up". Probably the latter. Don't get me wrong though, I like an upbeat, positive and can-do interview style. But if it is over-played, it can back-fire. Especially if it is not the real you (see the "actor" style, below). It depends on the function you play too. In some cases, perky will be just fine (see Disneyland Resort's Peter Pan character bio). In others, you won't be taken seriously. Even if you are you being you.

3. Slug – This one blows me away. The opposite of Perky, this person does not move a muscle. And I've been tempted in the past to stop the interview and start a therapy session. Because you absolutely have to show outward signs of being interested. And energetic. If you feel this might be you, please get some help. A career coach, a former boss or a good friend. Someone who can put you through a mock interview and provide you with some perspective. You can even call me!

4. Needy – I meet with a lot of job seekers and I understand how hard it has been on everyone and their families. I get that. But that cannot come across in an interview. You cannot say: "I really need this job". But people do. It says desperation. Even if you are feeling that, do everything you can to walk into an interview with confidence. Critical.

5. Actor – You really do need to be yourself in a job interview. If you got the interview despite a resume that doesn't exactly qualify you, be careful that you don't continue the charade in person. If you aren't a creative, don't pretend that you are. If you tend to be more of an independent worker, don't say "yes, absolutely" when asked if you love to lead cross-functional teams. You will be found out. Later in the process or a few weeks into the job. Not fun.

6. Funny – Everyone seems to know that cracking jokes is not real smart during an interview. With few exceptions, it just doesn't work. And the room isn't ready for it anyway. But some try to lighten the mood with other ways of being funny. Again, doesn't work. What can work and be even more interesting is to highlight your creativity, ingenuity and innovative ideas. I like that very much.

7. Cozy – Sure, take off your coat. Lean back. Rest your arm on the seat back of your chair. But be careful. While I want you comfortable and relaxed so I can see the real you, I don't want you too cozy. It suggests things. Most not intended. But interviewers are highly open to cues when across the desk. Watching for everything. Often because they don't really know what to ask (yes, it's true) and how to interpret what you've said against their internal criteria. Sad but true.

8. Chatty – Some like to meander during the answer to an interview question. Some just start off talking and can't stop. Hey we all get nervous. And those first 5 minutes are really an important time to establish yourself in the interview. Chatty often leads to irrelevant information exchange and time wasting. Whether you have 30 minutes or an hour, the minutes matter. Cadence matters. As well as getting into a good pattern.

9. Asker – I love good questions. A few early are fine. A follow-up here and there. And a few at the end to learn more about the company. After all, good interviews are two-way. A structured conversation. But too many questions can get really annoying. Especially in the first interview. If you are going to ask them, make sure they are relevant to the job and department. Not just a bunch of random inquiries to "show your interest" in the job.

10. Serious – Ever interview someone who never smiles? Interviews as if the world will be on their shoulders as soon as they are hired? The truth is most jobs aren't important enough to come in with this attitude. It suggests self-importance or over-preparedness. They forgot the last step prior to stepping in the interview room. To relax and be yourself. I'm not looking for big smiles for an hour. But let's keep things in perspective.

I think we have all leaned in to one of these styles depending on our situation. Whether a job seeker or hiring company market. And depending on where we are in our careers.

Especially today with so many folks out there looking. But even in the future (yes, there will be a future) when companies will be providing incentives for you to come work there.

No one wants to hire someone that makes them shiver. Or scream in the night.

CHAPTER DISCUSSION QUESTIONS

1. Which interview styles have you used?

2. Is there a style that does work most effectively?

3. Pick two styles. How do think interviewers react to these?

34

On Being A Good Fit

A round man cannot be expected to fit in a square hole right away. He must have time to modify his shape.

Mark Twain

Some say that the resume is about "qualifications" and the interview is about "fit". And it is true that the resume is a poor substitute for an in-person interview. And, really, until you meet someone it is really difficult to have any idea as to whether they will succeed at your company.

The professional resume is largely an objective tool. Although it can be reviewed subjectively. We can all choose to give candidates more or less credit for accomplishments. Based on our own lens and our reaction to the way a candidate writes their professional cover letter.

But the interview is where the interesting aspect of "fit" really begins to come into play.

And what is "fit" really? And how much influence do qualifications have in the final analysis?

Well the puzzle pieces above give you an idea, but those best represent the objective side, right? A company has a job and you have skills and experience that either match well or don't match well. Those are your qualifications for the job compared to the requirements for the job.

I think we all get that part. The part that can befuddle and confuse is the subjective "fit". The gut call that companies make once all final round candidates have proven their ability to do the job.

And we've all been second place for a big job at least once in our careers.

So what ends up being the criteria for this subjective decision? Here are my thoughts.

1. The first 5 minutes of an interview are critical. My first reaction to you matters. The way you introduce yourself, carry yourself and interact with me early on establishes a first impression. Your success in the first 5 minutes with each interview will greatly influence the decision. And let's face it. We're all a bit judgmental. That's our job for the hiring company.

2. Risk. This is related to your qualifications. If you are a 90% fit in a tough market, there will likely be a few 100% folks in the competitive set. And the only way you will be handed the office key is if your subjective fit value is high. Because that reduces the risk for the hiring manager. She can then say to her boss: "I know Tim is missing that one small piece in his background, but the referral and strong recommendation from Mike carries a lot of weight." or "Did you see what a great communicator he was during the interviews? We need more people like Tim here."

3. Work style and work philosophy also matter. How you do your job matters. How well you interact with fellow employees well above and below your level. Are you structured and process oriented or more free-flowing and reactive? This can make a difference in a candidate review.

4. Personality and social skills can play a role. The way you interact with interviewers, other employees and the person at the front desk can make a difference. Ask your network about the culture there. Are they looking for social butterflies or worker bees? And don't forget to identify what you are looking for. Be yourself and pay attention on interview day.

5. The conversational nature of your interviews can be a factor. Not everyone will allow you to get into a dynamic back and forth. Some interviewers force you to answer question after question. But if you can open the door to more of a business discussion vs. an "interview", you may learn a lot more about what type of candidate the company is really looking to hire. One small risk? Too much conversation can lead to the interviewer being left without enough data on you to convince others that you are the one.

Be yourself. Because if they hire you. Not some version of yourself. You'll be happy in the end.

CHAPTER DISCUSSION QUESTIONS

1. What does a good fit look like at your last company?

2. What cultural traits are you a good fit for?

3. What questions can you ask to determine if a company is a good fit for you?

There Will Be Tough Days

35

Surfing. Or When Things Get Slow

Progress is not an illusion, it happens,
but it is slow and invariably disappointing.

George Orwell

First, let's get something straight. I am not a surfer. Oh, I've tried. Long board or short board, I'm a miserable surfer. But as a creative person in the midst of a job search in 2007, I was always looking for analogies (ways to understand and cope with what I was going through). I thought this was especially helpful in job search since it is an irregular experience for most of us.

So, how is job search similar to surfing, you say? I see five similarities:

1. Skill
Surfing requires real skill and dedication. A skill that comes naturally to some and painfully to others. If you are good, it is obvious to other surfers. When you are not, you could be shunned or banned from the beach. The skills for job search include strategy, communications, humility and assertiveness. Without these skills you may not be banned but you will have limited support from your network.

2. Balance
It seems pretty obvious that standing on a board perched on a fast moving wave requires significant balance. For the job seeker, balance comes in a number of ways. You have to decide where to spend your time between networking lunches, job search boards, e-mail market-

ing, informational interviews, etc. Being out of balance means you are spending time doing the wrong things.

3. Experience

Surfers know the water, the beach and the weather. Over the years, they learn the patterns of the surf. Job search also requires knowledge of the landscape and it is painfully obvious if you are without this experience. Smart job seekers look for help from key folks in the job community – people such as recruiters, career coaches and other mentors.

4. Patience

While sitting on their boards, surfers are a patient bunch. They know the ocean and understand that waves come in "sets" – three or four at a time and then nothing for a period of time. In my experience, job opportunities reflect a similar pattern. During my four month search, I experienced a "set" about every four weeks. Coincidence? Maybe.

5. Decisiveness

Because a set comes along infrequently, a surfer has to be decisive. If you don't catch one in the set, you are left waiting for the next one. If you believe in the analogy for job search, another set will come and you can rest easy knowing it is out there – forming. If you have a strong sense of what you are looking for in your next job, the wave to catch will be obvious. Do not hesitate.

CHAPTER DISCUSSION QUESTIONS

1. How do you utilize down times during job search?

2. How do you decide whether a job is worth pursuing?

3. Where do you keep track of all the job opportunities?

36

Procrastination - Your Biggest Enemy?

Procrastination is opportunity's assassin.

Victor Kiam

Of course there are many things that can disable your job search. Some are in your control and some are not . . .

Some are debilitating and some simply frustrating.

The enemy on my mind now, however, is a sneaky one. Hard to control. And sometimes hard to see. It works quietly in the background like a computer virus. Chewing up memory and productivity.

Even the word sounds dastardly. The word is so full of consonants that it sounds like the gnashing of teeth.

"Procrastination"

Is this a problem for you? Are you sure?

It has been an issue for me in the past (you can read my other blog called Quixoting® to learn how I let 20 years go by before acting on my ideas). So when I saw an article on the topic in Scientific American Mind, I knew I had to tell you about it.

The great article was written by Trisha Gura called "I'll Do It Tomorrow" where she suggests that "procrastination is damaging the careers, health and savings accounts of millions of Americans".

I referred to this idea generally in my 30 Ideas book when I suggested you need to be careful of optimism. That too much optimism might prevent a healthy dose of productive fear from driving you to take action.

But procrastination is less about optimism and more about simply avoiding doing the things you know you need to do. Sometimes to your significant peril – as the article suggests.

And you also may say "Isn't the risk just the opposite? That we will act too often, over-communicate and be perceived as desperate?"

Yes. And I know what you are thinking. There are too many things to plan and balance during job search. And you are right.

So first some examples of where and when procrastination can cripple you in job search – if you do not act:

1. Creating a top notch resume and online brand (Linkedin, Twitter, Blogging)
2. Building a detailed budget for expenses during your transition
3. Drafting and implementing a solid job search strategy
4. Calling and following up with influential networking contacts
5. Getting to important networking events

Now there are many reasons people don't do these things. Sometimes there is a lack of knowledge. Pride can get in the way. And sometimes you forget that this job search market is completely different. That the old ways of job search won't work.

Some of these things are hard. They require skills that you may not have. And you hesitate. Then hesitation turns to "put off" and then put off becomes forgotten.

In the article, Gura provides some great tips on how to recognize when you are procrastinating. These steps, which characterize the process of procrastination, were provided by William Knaus – a clinical psychologist in Massachusetts:

- You have an activity with a deadline that comes with a reward if done well or a punishment if not done correctly.
- You view the activity negatively, as boring, unpleasant, threatening or confusing.
- You magnify the onerousness of the task while discounting the incentives for acting now.
- To avoid or relieve the discomfort, you substitute another activity such as daydreaming, "organizing" or just about anything involving a computer.
- You tell yourself that you will get to the task, perhaps tomorrow. Then, when tomorrow comes, you make up another excuse.

Boy these sound familiar. Do you think surfing the job search engines for hours a day is a symptom of a procrastination problem. I think so, yes. Seemingly productive yet highly inefficient. And an incredibly passive activity. A classic time waster if used beyond its value.

So, how do you battle this beast before it quietly takes your legs out from under you?

Take action. Build a specific plan. And surround yourself with really smart people who can help you through the aspects of job search that you find more daunting.

With a plan you have confidence that you are executing a well-thought out and objective strategy. And you can slice this plan into smaller tactical bites. Easier to execute = more likely to complete.

CHAPTER DISCUSSION QUESTIONS

1. Are you a procrastinator?

2. Why do you delay doing important things?

3. What steps could you take to get started on a big initiative?

37

Take A Productive Day Off

Life is a series of experiences, each one of which
makes us bigger, even though sometimes it is hard
to realize this. For the world was built to develop
character, and we must learn that the setbacks and grieves
which we endure help us in our marching onward.

Henry Ford

As job seekers, it is easy to get a bit full of ourselves. Not so much in an arrogant way. We just get caught up.

For good reason, our lives transform into a very self-directed effort. And the timing is right. No one is going to blame you. Because they know that this focus is part of the process of finding work.

But it also can be too much. It can cause you to become selfish, obsessive and often lose perspective.

So here's a simple idea to help break you out of this cycle in job search.

For one day, take the focus completely off your search. And focus it on the needs of your network.

Pick an event that you know and where people know you. Let the entire focus of that event be on how you can help others.

But, how, you say?

1. Walk in completely unprepared. No resume. No bio. No business card. Your goal is to be unencumbered with your own marketing materials. Not distracted by your normal mission.

2. Find the group manager, introduce yourself and ask them if there is anyone they know of who needs networking support in your industry or function. Someone who is struggling. And ask for an introduction.

3. Circle the room one time and look for three people who look uncomfortable, available and perhaps ready to leave. Walk up to each (one at a time) and introduce yourself. Ask them questions about what they are looking for in their next role, why they came to this event and how you might able to support their search.

4. Once you've met "the three", consider introducing them to each other. Encourage them to grab a coffee the next day to build a relationship beyond the quick introduction.

5. Consider bringing your Watchlyst™ and have a goal of adding five new people to it during the event. Make sure you get very specific information about their objectives.

Beyond the obvious value of helping others, there are a few really important benefits to you. This is the selfish part.

BENEFIT ONE - By taking the focus off of you for one day, you get a new perspective. You see new opportunities to do something good with your time "in between". And you can put a new, fresh energy to your search the next day.

BENEFIT TWO - People will see your effort and want to return the favor. The people you help. The people who notice you helping others. Including, perhaps, the group manager. Who needs volunteers for the next meeting? And volunteering gets you noticed within a group. You are now someone who knows how the group works and how someone new can learn the ins and outs of membership.

BENEFIT THREE - You create a positive image for yourself in the networking community. Then osmosis begins to occur as ideas, new friends and job opportunities begin to flow to you on a more regular basis. You attract the help of others.

And I'd suggest doing this once a month. Perhaps you pick a different event each time.

Of course there is a hybrid version of this. You can pick the first half of the day to be about others and the second half to be about your search effort. Or you can mix and mingle the two as is commonly done.

But I think the idea of taking the focus off of you for a full day makes sense. It will have a bigger impact on you and on the people you meet.

Give it a try. And pay attention for signs that it worked. For you and your network.

CHAPTER DISCUSSION QUESTIONS

1. Have you ever taken a day off during job search?

2. What would happen if you turned your attention to others?

3. What are the long-term benefits of serving other people?

38

101 (Other) Things To Do During Job Search

Your big opportunity may be right where you are now.
Napoleon Hill

Believe it or not, having other things on your mind besides job search helps clear your head. It allows you a few distractions so that you can stop checking e-mail every 10 minutes. Is that you?

I also believe very strongly that despite the stress and frustration that comes with an extended job search, there is a positive that must be recognized. That job search, despite its frustrations, can be a great opportunity. To take time for you and to appreciate the chance to get a few important things done.

So here's the list:

1. Walk or drive your kids to school
2. Coach your daughter's soccer team
3. Volunteer at church
4. Take a drive up the coast to visit family
5. Take a class at the local university
6. Give your dog a bath
7. Start a blog
8. Re-assess your priorities in life

9. Create a short term and long-term financial plan

10. Paint your house

11. Transfer VHS family movies to DVD

12. Take to your spouse or significant other to brunch

13. Pull the old guitar out of the attic and serenade someone

14. Research your family tree

15. Organize a family reunion

16. Organize your home filing system

17. Create an estate plan

18. Pursue an entrepreneurial dream

19. Locate an old family friend and write him or her a letter (on paper with a pen)

20. Write a poem

21. Go to the gym (everyday)

22. Cook healthy dinners

23. Go to a museum

24. Re-negotiate your home, life and auto insurance rates

25. Start a family Yahoo! Group

26. Organize your recipe cards

27. Train for a half marathon

28. Learn a foreign language

29. Teach a class at the local community college

30. Pick one person in your network and find them a job

31. Plan a neighborhood block party

32. Put on an elaborate puppet show for your kids (fun, colorful socks work great)

33. Read the Bible

34. Work in your child's classroom

35. Lose 10 pounds

36. Plant a garden

37. Go on long bike rides

38. Sand and re-paint an old piece of furniture

39. Replace all your light bulbs with the "green" kind

40. Recycle everything

41. Join a book club and actually read the assigned books

42. Install baseboards and crown molding

43. Try painting or carving something

44. Write a thank you note to an inspirational high school or college teacher

45. Meet your local congressional representative

46. Start a 529 plan for your kids (even if contributions may come slow)

47. Get a physical and depending on your age or gender, key disease screeners

48. Have your kids fingerprinted

49. Walk your dog… everyday

50. Write a business plan for a friend

51. Clean out all of your closets and donate the extras to charity

52. Organize a food drive for the local food bank

53. Play handyman (or woman) for an elderly neighbor

54. Order and analyze your credit report

55. Do your own taxes

56. Play chess in the park

57. Make your lawn the envy of the community

58. Be like Clark Griswold and light up your Christmas

59. Make a video interview of yourself so people can see and hear your 100 years from now

60. Go on long hikes and think about what working people are doing right then

61. Plan an economical boys or girls night out (this way you know you can afford it)

62. Clean out your rain gutters

63. Join a free online fantasy sports league

64. Write a patent

65. Catch a matinee – preferably an old western or love story

66. Become an active alumni of your college or Greek organization

67. Go to a senior center and read someone the newspaper

68. Set up a Flickr account and organize all your photos

69. Write an ebook and give it away for free

70. Go to the library (a quiet place to get away from the phone)

71. Wash dishes by hand

72. Read a different magazine every day for 30 days (library)

73. Write your goals and, if married, share them with your spouse

74. Bake cookies once a week

75. Use the BBQ (again, once a week)

76. Smile at people you meet

77. Wash your windows

78. Check all your smoke detectors

79. Test for mold in your home

80. Insulate your doors and windows (saves $)

81. Become a Big Brother or Big Sister

82. Build a cool lemonade stand for your kids

83. Frame and hang important family pictures

84. Get new house keys made (before they break)

85. Write a letter to a service person fighting in Iraq

86. Look for five ways to save money around the house

87. Plan a family slumber party (including tents) in the living room

88. Join the board of directors for a local charity

89. Be a volunteer for the next NPR station membership drive

90. Sleep in during the week (once a month)

91. Go fishing with an old friend

92. Sell extra "treasure" on eBay

93. Stop smoking. Really.

94. Create an iMovie or a fun slideshow on iPhoto

95. Buy a finch feeder and watch nature for a few minutes each day

96. Have a garage sale

97. See a free play at a local school or park

98. Catch a local little league game (and grab a hot dog and coke to go with it)

99. Smother your family with all the attention they've been missing

100. Go camping or take another inexpensive vacation

101. Take a deep breath and be grateful for everything you have.

Whew! So, what's my point? If you never have another extended break in your career, what will you wish you did during this period?

While you can't do it all – clearly your #1 priority is to be and remain focused on networking yourself into that next job – make sure some of what you do is more nourishing than frustrating.

CHAPTER DISCUSSION QUESTIONS

1. What if this ends up being your only career break?

2. Will you wish you did more with the time and flexibility?

3. What would be on your list?

39

Light A Candle

How far that little candle throws its beams!
So shines a good deed in a naughty world.
William Shakespeare

Job search by candlelight struck me as a compelling way to think about the contemplative nature of the job search experience.

Not everyone in job search mode grapples with the experience. Many relish the chance to engage in battle with others. They look to be the last one standing.

But most of us have our trying moments along the way. Sometimes we burn brighter. And sometimes we burn low at risk of burning out.

So I started thinking about other times when life by candlelight forces us to think more clearly about our situation. It doesn't always have to be serious thinking, but the situation clearly asks more of us. It asks us to suspend our arguably more casual and flippant nature. We tend to joke and make light of things in life – especially when we are a bit nervous.

But when the candle is lit, something happens. For some reason, the candlelight tricks us into thinking more deeply about our lives. Kind of like a visual truth serum. Not forceful. Rather, the candlelight draws the honesty out of us.

So, for example:

> ...Visualize folks in New England after an ice storm trying to figure out how to keep the community warm.

> ...Consider a church altar filled with flickering light as a family struggles with thoughts of a sick loved one.

> ...Picture a group of friends huddled around a small dinner table, sharing the good times of their high school memories with a bottle of red wine.

> ...Stop and remember the feeling of driving past a roadside memorial, the candles still burning low in the glass.

> ...Preview in your mind a Valentine's Day dinner this week at a local Italian restaurant, holding hands with someone you love.

You'll have to agree, those are some pretty honest moments. You are not calculating how you will feel. You are just feeling.

Job search, in my opinion, has that same kind of power. It asks you to conserve, to focus and to act with purpose. It creates a sense of urgency in your life. It forces a time line into your life – one that stops the clock and allows you a significant chunk of time to take stock. To have an honest review of who you are, what you do and where you are going.

While you are actively looking for a job, I hope that you are also contemplating life. If, for some reason, losing your job via lay off or restructuring is not a humbling and thoughtful moment in your life, perhaps you should consider making it so.

Interested?

Tonight, after you get back to the house, grab a candle. Clear off a table somewhere in your house (the bigger the room the better) of everything and place the candle right in the middle. Place a pad of paper and a pen on the table. Turn off all the lights and light the candle. Now leave the room for 5 minutes. Use the restroom, wash your face, brush your teeth – whatever you need to get settled. As you walk back into the room, pay attention to the light as it reflects off the corners and edges of the room.

Sit down and write down what's happening in your head. "I'm excited. I'm afraid. I'm cautious. I'm optimistic." But most important, be thoughtful. What will you do with this time off? Even if it is time you'd rather spend earning money, allow yourself a chance to think during your time in between jobs.

Now go right to bed. No TV or radio to interfere with the true reality show you just produced.

So I am asking you to manufacture an honest moment. Because, for some reason, candles bring out the best in us. And you need your best when important things are on the line.

CHAPTER DISCUSSION QUESTIONS

1. What does your contemplative time look like?

2. Where can you go to think and reflect on this time in life?

3. What is the benefit of a few honest moments during job search?

Momentum Can Be Elusive

40

Light A Bonfire

It is not light that we need, but fire;
it is not the gentle shower, but thunder.
We need the storm, the whirlwind, and the earthquake.
Frederick Douglass

In chapter 39 I asked to light a candle - here we're talking about a much bigger flame! You see there's something about a big bonfire that gets us going. That stirs something in us.

Do you remember big bonfire moments in your life?

1. A high school or college rally the night before the big football game.

2. A beach party celebrating the end of summer

3. The closing event for a sleep over camp up in the mountains

Bonfires stimulate in so many ways that they can't help but stoke your senses. And give you a powerful feeling of being in the moment.

- the searing heat: no matter how close you sit, you can feel it like small pins on your cheeks

- the bright glare: big and growing flames that drink up the oxygen

- the exploding sounds: loud pops and crackles as embers snap

And in job search it seems like you need to light a fire. To clear your mind. To energize your body and to drive purposeful action.

But it can be especially helpful when you are heading into an important week. An interview with a target company. To focus your attention. And to prepare your mind.

The problem is that some weeks it is hard to get the fire started. You are often kneeling in the sand, knees being scraped by the rock and debris. Rubbing two sticks together and not getting any heat. Not even a wisp of smoke on which to blow to flame.

But you have to keep trying.

Because if you start your week the way you always do – sitting at the computer – you are likely to end up the same way at the end of the week.

Sitting at the computer wondering where all the job leads are. And wondering why no one has called you back.

So how do you kick off your week off in a big way?
With confidence? And with a purpose?

Well, you light a big fire, of course. Here's how:

1. Get your kindling together – You need the right wood to create a good fire. A dry wood that burns hot and big. In job search, what creates a good fire is the right marketing tools. Examples include a strong resume and cover letter, elevator pitch, networking bio and business cards. Need some new ideas? You can find your kindling all in one place via the free downloads at timsstrategy.com.

3. Invite a crowd – You can't have a great bonfire without a crowd. And if you haven't created a network that cares, you have some work to do. To keep yourself top of mind. And once you have, you need to invite them to the party. Send out a note this week to your network. Reminding them that you are still out here. That you need their help. And make sure they are reminded of your specific job search objectives.

4. Generate oxygen – You do this every week in the way that you network – by helping others. By connecting people. And by physically getting out of the house where people can find you. And where your candidacy for new jobs can take in a big deep breath.

5. Light a match – What ignites the kindling is your mind-set. A belief in yourself and in the knowledge that you can do great things. Because if you can't back up your materials with confidence, your materials will fall flat. A great resume gets the phone interview. But a lack of confidence or an inability to tell your great story simply gets you the door (your exit).

6. Keep it going – Like any good flame, this one needs to be fed. With strong thank you notes to your network. With follow-ups (things you promised to do for others). With updates and improvements to your marketing materials. And by adding new contacts every week to your list.

Well, what are you waiting for? This fire won't light itself, right?

CHAPTER DISCUSSION QUESTIONS

1. How can you get a fire burning in your search?

2. Do you have a crowd around you to enjoy and appreciate the fire?

3. How will you create the spark to keep going each week?

41

Keep The Ball Rolling

The time for action is now.
It's never too late to do something.
Antoine de Saint-Exupery

In business and in life, momentum is a wonderful thing. Once you have it, there is inertia and a magnetic quality that seems to draw additional opportunities to you.

But it's more than a magical magnetism. Less mysterious than a cosmic tractor beam. And there are ways to feed momentum so that the ball keeps rolling. And good things keep happening to you.

Here are six ways:

1. You have to believe that it will happen. And that you are deserving of it happening. Not that this belief will trigger the world to act on your behalf. But rather that you are able to project confidence. And expecting good things to happen in your job search effort. I know this sounds a bit like believing in secret scrolls, but if it positively affects your attitude, it is a good thing. And it will be painfully obvious to others if your self-confidence is lacking.

2. You have to remove any impediments. Things that will physically or mentally slow you down. Or distract you. A good analogy here is going for a run with a dog. I always thought this was a great idea. Me and my dog Casey out for a run on a beautiful Saturday AM. Man and his best friend jogging joyfully in the park.

Except it didn't work. Because my dog gets distracted by other dogs, by every tree we pass and the rabbit that crosses on the trail. So we never really get going and I never get a good run in. So these represent impediments or things that get in the way of a good result. And slow your momentum. For job search, these include not having a good elevator pitch, not knowing how to introduce yourself to new people or not having good marketing materials (a one sheet bio and business card for networking).

3. You need to build a network that cares about you. A network that has you "top of mind" vs. "bottom shelf". You do that through selfless efforts to support the folks you meet, asking great questions to learn what they need/care about, by telling them specifically about your job search objectives, by becoming a person of influence and finally by simply being a good networker.

4. You need to remain visible. People can't help you or remember that you are still in the market if they don't see or hear from you. Get out of the house for a minimum of 4 hours per day. Schedule coffees, attend networking events, get out to events where you can network with employed people (not just the unemployed). Send a regular network update via e-mail that quickly reminds people of your objectives. Tell them in that note the good things that are happening. And that you'd like their help to keep the momentum going!

5. You need fresh new leads every week. Fresh new leads are the food of momentum. And the more you have in the hopper, the better. I call it the power of multiple options. It allows you to focus on more than one opportunity with confidence. Because you are not hyper-focused on one job opening. And desperate to convince someone that you are the only one they should be interviewing. Whether at the job offer stage or the phone interview stage, you can now be yourself knowing that everything isn't riding on this one position.

6. You can feel free to ask good, probing questions. To help you understand if the job is really a good fit for you. Fresh new leads come from your network. Especially a network that already has tangible data on your job search objectives. You can get leads from Indeed, Monster and other online job search engines. You can also get them from company websites, networking organizations or churches that have a job search group on Yahoo. You just need a steady flow to keep your spirits up.

CHAPTER DISCUSSION QUESTIONS

1. What's keeping you from building momentum?

2. How can you stay visible to your network?

3. Where are you getting new, fresh leads?

42

Building On Small Wins

If it doesn't matter who wins or loses,
then why do they keep score?

Vince Lombardi

Creating momentum in job search can be hard. Carving out a few victories along the way is a big part of creating it. And you know what can be really hard? Recognizing them as victories when they may seem really small against your larger objective of finding that next great role.

I wanted to share some examples of victories that your fellow job seekers have shared in a great discussion. On my Linkedin group.

So, here they are. 10 examples of small victories:

1. **A new connection.** Some days these can seem really small, but each connection will lead to something. And it is something new to pursue.

2. **A phone interview.** Maybe you got it via connections on Linkedin. Perhaps a vendor friend from a prior job helped you get it.

3. **An e-mail response.** You finally heard back from that company you submitted to a month ago. No matter the answer, hopefully something was resolved or cleared up.

4. **An informational interview.** Not only did you learn something new about a target company or industry, but you just might have given someone a reason to forward your resume on to someone else.

5. **A phone call.** Maybe it was a recruiter. Maybe it was an old college friend who works in an industry you've been targeting.

6. **A chance meeting.** Someone in the line at Starbucks. On an elevator. At the grocery store.

7. **A few new ideas.** Perhaps they were suggestions for a new job site to check out. A new recruiter in your industry. A job search blog (hey, good idea!).

8. **A short term consulting assignment.** This means some money in your wallet and a chance to keep your skills fresh. Consulting can be a great interim victory if you understand the pros and cons of consulting.

9. **A chance to volunteer.** Yes, you can do something good with your time off. And think of all the new people you'll meet! Whether you are stuffing envelopes for your local church or building a regional marketing plan for the local United Way, you put yourself in a target rich environment. Lots of new possible connections.

10. **Take a friend.** Have a friend who is a little shy? Bring them with you to your next networking event or one-on-one coffee meeting. It is a victory to help others. You've nudged them along and given them a reason to help you next time.

The key to all of these small victories though is that you have to be engaged. You have to be pro actively creating a situation in which others want to help you. Be an opportunistic extrovert. Eric from my Linkedin group is a great example. He shared a win story about waiting for his car at the dealer.

Eric did not get new connections by sitting on the comfy coach reading a car magazine, sipping free coffee and swallowing a few donuts. He looked around the room and took action. And made a few friends.

Now maybe Eric is unique you say. Freakishly outgoing with no fear. Well, that's just silly. All of us have some trepidation in networking. None are free of the nerves or ego restrictions that prevent starting a new conversation with a total stranger. Especially in an environment (like a car dealer) where most people are there for two reasons.

To get in and get out.

And with as little pain as possible on the wallet. And they don't even know that they could be a key contact for you in your quest to find something new.

But if you say "yes" to everything during job search. Especially to those opportunities that you might normally shy away from, you will create energy. And that energy will lead to small victories.

And once you have one, you can share it.

Sharing those victories builds momentum. Both real inertia and the kind that keeps your confidence up. When you really need it.

CHAPTER DISCUSSION QUESTIONS

1. What small wins can you count since your job search began?

2. Who are you sharing your wins with?

3. What can you learn from the wins of others in your network?

43

One Day In Job Search

*The best thing about the future is
that it comes one day at a time.*

Abraham Lincoln

The inspiration for this idea came from the song "One Day" by Mati-syahu. It is here to show you how each day in job search connects to the next.

One day a call will come from a networking friend. Someone I've shared coffee with and someone who knows my job search objectives. Turns out that a job has opened up with one of my target companies.

One day my resume will be walked into a hiring manager whose eyes will sparkle as they read about my background.

One day I will get a call from that same company who thinks I might be a good fit for their new position. They will be right.

One day the phone will ring and I will interview with a person in human resources. Someone who I connect with. And they will push me through to a first round interview.

One day I will walk with confidence up to a big door. One of my target companies. As I enter, I will have a good feeling about this one.

One day I will meet and interview with the people that will be my new associates from 8-5. I see myself working closely with them to make great things happen there.

One day someone will call and ask whether I have references. And my heart will jump.

One day I will wonder why things are taking so long. I will be impatient. But I won't show it.

One day I will be tempted to follow-up a second and third time. But I won't. I will let it linger.

One day I will get a call. And a job offer. The company will ask me to join them. I will be their top candidate. And they will want me to start as soon as I can.

One day I will put down the phone, walk into the other room and share the news. Hey, guess what?

One day I will send an announcement to my network. I will have arrived at a new job. And I will tell them my story. How I did it. And I will offer to help them.

One day I will turn off the alerts from Indeed.com

One day my resume will be a quiet file on my laptop. Back to the obscurity. Buried deep in a folder called my2011jobsearch.

One day I will stop attending networking events four days a week and sometimes in the evenings. Instead I will be home more often playing with my kids or enjoying a movie with my spouse or friends.

One day my life will be back in balance. I will be part of a new team as a leader or key contributor.

One day my pockets will again be full and the savings will start to peak ahead to a better day.

One day I will miss this challenge. This opportunity to prove myself. And compete with other great people.

One day I will realize that I am a better person as a result of this job search process. I will have learned about what I can do in difficult times. And I will appreciate all the new friends I've met.

And, **one day**, I will pull up to a new parking spot. At a new building. I will walk to the door and grab the handle. And smile.

One day...

CHAPTER DISCUSSION QUESTIONS

1. Can you see the connection between each day during job search?

2. Can you imagine the snowball effect of multiple days coming together?

3. Do you see the role of your networking in making this happen?

The Final Stretch

44

The Power Of Multiple Options

As a child my family's menu consisted of two choices: take it or leave it.

Buddy Hackett

In job search as in life, there is real power in having multiple options. A few choices to make.

Now, some may find this stressful. After all, is it easier to navigate our lives if we have fewer choices to make? Not for me. I like the decision process. And the moments that surround it.

I like that moment in life where we get to make a very substantial decision that will impact the entire path our life takes.

Those decisions include:

1. Where you go to college
2. The major you pursue
3. What first job you take out of high school or college
4. Whether you go back to school for an MBA or other advanced degree
5. Who you decide to marry
6. Whether to have kids
7. What city you call home
8. Which jobs you pursue during your career

Because each decision you make tosses you right into the middle of a new crowd. People that will influence you.

Can you think of one or two decisions that completely changed your life? Ever wonder what your life would look like had you made a different choice there? If you married Mary Sue vs. Tina? Mike instead of Butch?

So the power comes in the knowledge that you have. The knowledge that you are in a position to choose. In job search, the ability to choose from a few options during your process gives you confidence. And a sense of freedom.

And I'm not talking specifically about having multiple job offers. While that's nice and certainly has clear advantages, I'm talking about smaller choices and opportunities.

It's not about finding one thing. It is about generating multiple options. Constantly. Then the one job (the right one) will become more obvious.

Because if you have a constant effort to drum up new options, you will likely put yourself in a position where one opportunity (no matter how great) will not be your only choice. The freedom that comes from having a few things to choose from allows you to relax a bit.

Being relaxed allows you to be (and appear) more confident. It makes me want to talk with you and perhaps move you on to the next round of interviews.

If you are, however, looking at only one option. All the time. That option will seem magical. Something you can't let get away.

So you pursue it. Perhaps with too much passion. Maybe you look a bit desperate.

By having multiple options, you are allowed to pursue it quietly. With purpose. Because you know that if it doesn't work out, you have a few others to pursue. And, in fact, when you have multiple options you can be the pursued – not the pursuer. And there is power in that too.

So how do you generate multiple options? You work your network and use it to build a pipeline. A pipeline that will continually deliver new options to you.

CHAPTER DISCUSSION QUESTIONS

1. What's in your pipeline today?

2. What are you doing to generate new leads and opportunities each week?

3. What's the ongoing psychological value of having multiple options?

45

Thoughts On Negotiating An Offer

*There can be no settlement of a great cause without
discussion, and people will not discuss a cause
until their attention is drawn to it.*

William Jennings Bryan

Reading the title of this chapter may bring a couple of reactions.

1. An offer feels like a far away concept right now.

2. How did Tim know I was looking at an offer?

3. Negotiating? In this economy, is that even possible?

But the reality is that at some point you will get one. And, of course, you need to be ready. There is a free tool on the site called SideBySide™. This tool is designed to help you evaluate a job offer. To look at it objectively when you may be in the least objective position (i.e. ready for this job search to end and open to anything that will provide a solution).

Now that you've done an objective evaluation, you have a choice to make. You can (A) accept the offer or (B) you can begin a discussion about how the offer might be re-arranged or improved somehow. And, while I would not advise you to simply accept an offer without a discussion, I would not beat you up for doing so in a tough economy. Especially if your financial situation is dire or if the offer is actually pretty close to your objectives.

You can spoil a great interview and offer process by being a sour negotiator. One who holds back acceptance on small, rather insignificant points. Yes, it's true that "if you don't ask, you don't get". It's also true that you are unlikely to negotiate much after you start on day one. But I think it matters what you ask for, why you ask for it and how that request is delivered.

One more reason this is an important discussion. One that should be well-thought out.

This is your first real strategic discussion with your new boss and/or new company.

It will set the tone for your transition into the new organization. Others will find out if your negotiation was strong and confident vs. petty and ill-conceived. That matters.

So here are my five thoughts:

1. Know Your Situation

One of the keys will be really understanding your situation. Being able to objectively review where you are financially, psychologically and physically. You may say: "I'm done. It has been 9 months and I just can't do it any more." You may also say: "While I am ready to get back to work, I need to make sure that in this negotiation I stand-up for myself and ask for what I deserve. I am OK if it means that I need to keep looking." Whatever your situation, be aware of it. Know your financials. And importantly, know the perspective of your family. Even if you are ready to negotiate hard, how does your spouse feel about that?

2. Ask Questions

From a hiring manager's perspective, asking questions says something important about you. It says that you are thoughtful. That you are not impulsively asking for more money simply because that sounds like the right thing to do. Asking questions allows you to gain critical information about the situation of the company overall and perhaps may give you some insight as to how you might be able to create a "win-win" for both parties.

3. Get Creative

Let's face it, a negotiation can go a number of different ways. And this is your last significant interaction with the company and its staff prior to potentially becoming a part of it. You want to leave a positive lasting impression. Because once the letter is signed, you need to shift into "adding value" mode. And you can kick off this new relationship in a good way be being creative now. Offering the company some unique ways to satisfy your needs in a way that works for them. A way that perhaps was not on their list but would be an acceptable substitution. Say, for example, and education allowance or small car allowance instead of a salary increase.

4. Simplify

Sometimes we do all the right things. We brainstorm ten different ideas. Some big and some small. All things in an offer letter we'd like to change, add or remove. And then that great brainstorm turns into a request. You ask for all of it. And in some economies, that might work. In this one and in the average economy, it won't. And it may backfire on you. So I suggest you simplify. Pick one or two important things based on your situation and supported by the company's answers to your questions. Focus on those two things. If you get them both, great! If you get one, make sure you can feel good having received that adjustment.

5. What Matters

In the end, you really have to think big picture. Long term. Is it really about salary for you? Is there a number you absolutely must have that you will fight to the end for? Fall on your sword? Or are you at a point in your career where education assistance is really most important. Building your skills through a degree, advanced degree or series of seminars. Knowing where you are in your career and what matters to you is important. And it will also be important to the company. If your request is purely selfish (and there is nothing wrong with asking respectfully for what you believe you are worth), you will potentially get a different reaction. If you are asking for something that helps you and supports your ability to grow or improve the company, well that can help. But what matters most to you?

And one last point. Negotiate, where possible, in person. Across the desk.

Your presence helps to create a sense of urgency for both parties and allows for a more personable discussion. So now it is up to you. You get to decide.

CHAPTER DISCUSSION QUESTIONS

1. Are you comfortable with a negotiation? Why or why not?

2. Do you know what really matters to you in an offer?

3. How can you simplify your needs for a decision maker?

46

Ways To Celebrate Your Arrival

Let us celebrate the occasion with wine and sweet words.

Plautus

When you find your new job. And you will. You can do one of two things.

1. You can view your arrival with a stoic face. And say to yourself: "Job well done". Nary a wink or bright smile there, but it fits your personality. And is consistent with your careful approach to living this part of your life.

2. You can celebrate. I'm not suggesting you celebrate with a rave of epic proportions. But rather a proper celebration of this time in your life. To recognize its impact on your career. And to take a few minutes to appreciate those around you that have played a role in your transition.

Some of you may wonder about the use of the word "arrival" since almost everyone uses "landing or landed" to describe their escape from the job search process. I've always preferred the term "arrival" since "landing" sounds like you've just returned from a bumpy flight.

And while that may better describe your job search journey, to me "arriving" sounds more like something to celebrate. Recognition of your completing a successful effort. Having learned a few things along the way. And allowing yourself to be changed by the experience.

So, when the day comes, here are four ways you can celebrate your arrival at a new job in style:

1. Send out a new job arrival announcement

Most of you know to do this. And most of you know to wait until at least your first day. In case of a last minute snafu with the new job, offer or position. But once you are sure (few weeks), send out a note to introduce your new role and company to everyone who played a role in your job search. Everyone loves sending this announcement. And you should. It feels good.

2. Share your experience with others

Your job search has taught you a lot. You made mistakes. And learned from them. You would be amazed just how much time you can save others by writing down your best practices. Resources that helped you. And your view on what events, tools or services are worth paying for. I created a free download on the site to help you do this. I called it Shortcuts™. It is pass-along career advice. Because if you do a good job you will help more people than you think. Good stuff gets passed around.

3. Recognize and thank your network

Of course you can do this in your announcement and to some extent in your version of ShortCuts. But I am guessing that there are 20-30 people who played a bigger role. And it's hard to include everyone on an e-mail. So what about having a party at your house. Or at a local restaurant. I'm not saying you even have to buy everyone dinner. Maybe plan a time around happy hour. Where you can recognize those who helped you succeed. And personally thank them for their support in finding a new job.

4. Take your family away for the weekend

These are the ones who were there with you along the way. The ones that heard you get upset on bad days and hoped along with you that the right hiring manager saw what you thought you showed in each interview. Those who never quite knew what you did every day. But were in your corner the whole time. It doesn't have to be an expensive trip. And if times are tight you can make it one night. Or one long day.

In the end, your recognition of this time in life is important. Regardless of which of the above options you consider.

And finishing it with a celebration will end it all on a positive note. A positive note you can maintain by offering your services for those still looking. Going to networking events, being a connector and making yourself available for job seekers looking to meet someone like you.

And then you can be there to celebrate their arrival. You'll be a pro.

CHAPTER DISCUSSION QUESTIONS

1. What is the right way to celebrate your arriving at a new job?

2. Who should you include in your celebration?

3. How much time should you ask for between saying "yes" and your first day?

47

A Nod To Your Freedom

Freedom is nothing but a chance to be better.
Albert Camus

The last chapter was about how you can celebrate your arrival in a new job. So you can plan for it. And not forget to recognize those who helped make it happen. Or suffered miserably by your side.

Maybe you can bookmark these pages for when the big day comes.

This chapter is about recognizing the affect of this job search experience. As Ricky Bobby famously said in Talladega Nights: "That just happened".

But more important perhaps is to allow yourself some time to look back over the journey. And find moments to relish. The days you helped others find a job. The interviews you nailed. And the new friends you encountered each week.

Because your life will change. A good thing, yes.

But recognize that you will need to adjust. There will be a few things to miss. Even if, as we all know, we'd rather have the job and miss a few things than struggle to find work. Right?

Here are a few things you might miss:

1. The hours - There's a real freedom that comes with job search. You work the hours necessary to succeed. I'm not saying job search takes fewer hours. But some weeks it can take less. And then you have options.

2. Being the CEO - You are the only person running your job search franchise. And that can be liberating. You plan your days, who you meet with and where you invest your money.

3. Spending time with family - One of the blessings of a job search transition is the opportunity to catch up on some much needed family time. No set schedule and no commute means you can walk your kids to school, have lunch with your spouse and be a contributing member of the family more often than when you were working full time.

In fact some of these will be so valuable that a part of you won't want to go back quite so soon. You may look for ways to extend the benefits of transition. So be ready for that bitter-sweet aspect. I felt it.

Some of you will toss everything related to your job search once you've arrived at the new job. And find a dark closet to store your job search binder, fancy interview clothes and resume paper.

But I will miss you. Interacting with readers is what makes my work rewarding. It's one of the reasons I'm writing about issues beyond job search (career and life).

With hopes that you'll stick around. Just so you know.

CHAPTER DISCUSSION QUESTIONS

1. What will you miss about your transition period?

2. What will be your biggest issue with transitioning back into a company?

3. How will you work to maintain your network?

48

Be Awesome In Everyday Life

The moment one gives close attention to any thing,
even a blade of grass it becomes a mysterious, awesome,
indescribably magnificent world in itself.

Henry Miller

So it's comfortable to coast through life. In fact it is downright easy.

Like a leaf floating down the edge of a slow moving river. It bumps along a few rocks along the way. Sometimes it gets caught in one place for a few minutes. Then it is freed and continues its passive journey.

Then it is violently thrown over the edge of a huge cliff, propelled downward by a billion drops of water. And crushed to watery final grave.

Depressing, I know.

Ever feel like this leaf?

In a weird way, being laid off, fired or otherwise separated is like someone lifting you out of that slow moving stream. Let's face it, most careers are not leading to the white house, the executive floor or even a corner office.

So despite it being an unwanted event, you now have an opportunity. To be something different. To change your approach. And to try some new things.

But instead of just stuff to be doing, what qualifies for awesome?

After all, you have a bit of time to think about what you do each day. And you have time to execute it well.

So here are 3 ways you can be awesome:

1. Expose A Great (But Less Known) Person To A Lot Of New People – This is a way to use your influence (and we all have some influence) to help out someone younger or less exposed. It feels great to receive this kind of a gift. Because after you've worked hard on something, it feels great to have it recognized by someone around or above you. The CEO who hears about a client service person going out of their way to help a customer. And highlighting that person in front of the entire company. The social media superstar with billions of followers who re-tweets a great post by a little known writer. The restaurant customer who so appreciates a server or chef that they tip big and go online to tell the world of their amazing experience.

2. Take Action On Your Ideas And Pay Attention To Your Inner Voice – I spoke recently to a person I met at a recent presentation. She was calling to get a few leads for her target companies. But our call ended up focusing on her real passion. A former dietitian, she has bounced around a few industries. But now she has (I can hear it) a need to morph into someone new. She has a specific plan to use her joy of cooking to build a business. And I told her my story of taking action on my ideas. That I never truly knew what to do until I took action. And paid attention to how it felt to do so. What's awesome is the real you. Instead of the one that followed the pack out of college. So when you do this, you drip awesome. The world needs more people doing what they are meant to do. You'll be happier at work as a result.

3. When You Are Somewhere, Be There 100% – You can't be awesome if you are not giving yourself fully. Now I will tell you that I am still "becoming" in this one. It is hard to focus when your head won't stop swimming with ideas. And impulses. But the people who I find awesome? They capture my attention by giving me theirs. Real eye contact, super active listening, a good smile and an obvious interest in my answers to their questions. It's like getting licked by 10 cute puppies. Feels good.

So pick one of the three above and find something you can do when inspired. To be awesome.

Or I guess you can just float along. Getting your legs wet.

CHAPTER DISCUSSION QUESTIONS

1. What are you inspired to do?

2. What good can you do each week to help other people?

3. What does it feel like to see others benefit from your help?

49

How To Enable A Positive Attitude In Life

Your living is determined not so much by what
life brings to you as by the attitude you bring to life;
not so much by what happens to you as by the way
your mind looks at what happens.

Khalil Gibran

It's hard to hide from a smiling face. Especially when the eyes on that smiling face find yours.

Aren't we highly attracted to a smile?

I'll bet if you were asked to walk through a warehouse of people, you would naturally find the smiling faces over the ones without expression.

Are you smiling now?

And when was the last time you had a good laugh?

Here's an interesting little task: Take out a piece of paper and write down five things that get you smiling. I wonder how many of you will get five.

If you did, how many of them are manufactured smiles? Triggered by a You Tube video or a comedy sketch. To me, those smiles aren't worth as much. While I'll never turn down a good smile or laugh, I prefer the ones that occur naturally. As a result of things being more right than not in your life.

So how would you like to start smiling without being provoked?

How? By enabling a positive attitude in life. By making changes in your life's focus, habits and environment.

So here a few ways to get you started:

1. Stay busy

Some psychologists believe that keeping the mind busy is the best way to stay positive. Read this from Mihaly Csikszentmihalyi, a Hungarian psychology professor:

"With nothing to do, the mind is unable to prevent negative thoughts from elbowing their way to center stage . . . worries about one's love life, health, investments, family, and job are always hovering at the periphery of attention, waiting until there is nothing pressing that demands concentration."

So if you are not pro actively staying busy, your mind wants to head south. And your attitude goes with it. While we all need down time, make sure to fill that down time with positive activities.

2. Be around positive people

OK, here's another list. Write down five names. The people who make up the bulk of your social life. Whether during the work week or on the weekends. Give each of them a score from 1-10 (1 = very negative, 10 = very positive). Then add up the scores and divide by five.

Is this a silly exercise? Can you really score your friends on their positive attitude? Sure you can. Think about your last few conversations. Are these people strikingly positive or not so much?

3. Do something that matters to you

Acting with a sense of purpose in life provides a constant and supportive background. Like a constant green screen behind you. Projecting and reinforcing the things that matter. But if your purpose is resting comfortably in a bottom drawer somewhere, you will see the opposite effect.

Not acting on your ideas. Not pursuing a passion. Both will leave you frustrated and repressed.

Not sure what matters to you? Pick three things that might matter and take a few simple steps toward them. Pay attention to the way you feel when working on each. Do it long enough and you'll know.

4. Open up in social media

Are you scared to really share anything of interest with the social media world? Do you step into the online water as if it were burning hot, liquid magma? You may not share a photo on LinkedIn or Twitter. And are not really engaging anyone in discussions. Not really.

So it is time to break out. To be yourself. And to enjoy the social soup. If you do, you'll feel more connected to the world around you. And make way for your more positive attitude.

5. Do what you love as often as you can

We all have natural talents. Things we are built to do. And then we add on additional skills as necessary to complete our total package for an employer or client.

We are happy at work and most positive in life when we spend the bulk of our day creating value. And it almost feels effortless. Because we love doing it.

6. Let go and do a few uncomfortable things

Afraid to do something in life? Take a small risk and jump into something new. There is a natural energy that comes with putting yourself in a new environment. If you regulate your life too much by limiting its scope, you will miss out on chances to grow. To change. And become.

CHAPTER DISCUSSION QUESTIONS

1. What small risk can you take today to enable a positive attitude?

2. What do you love to do more than anything?

3. Do you have too much thinking time? How could you fill that time with something valuable?

Acknowledgments

There are a number of people that deserve recognition for this book's completion:

To my wife Michele, my kids and all of our friends in Southern California for supporting my writing, ideating and creating.

To my Mom who passed away in 2008, thank you for your sense of right. Your beautiful reminders to be yourself and to go grab things you want in life. I promise to use your gifts for good.

To my Dad who passed away in 2009, thank you for the desire to write and share ideas. For a love of cars and sports. And for being a struggling entrepreneur who tried so many cool things. No matter the outcome.

To Lani Merlina (http://merlinadesign.com) for the layout of this book, logo creation, design and all other graphics used in my life!

To Matt Crane (http://c4development.com) for all his help on the technical side of the blog and website. All things that work are a credit to Matt's skill and experience in software. Anything that doesn't work? My fault.

To Neal Schaffer (http://windmillnetworking.com) who I mention in the book (P. 70-71) for being a great expert in social media (LinkedIn, Twitter and the like). He's also a great friend and fellow blogger. My weekly meetings with Neal provide a burst of energy and ideas each and every time.

To Thom Singer (thomsinger.com) who reappeared after 20 years to become a big influence in my blogging and speaking efforts. Thanks for offering a great example for others to follow.

To bloggers everywhere that I meet at Blog World, South By Southwest or at the great networking events in Southern California. Thanks for inspiring me with your writing and for sharing what's been working for you.

To career experts around the world, thanks for being a part of my career expert directory, for sharing my ideas on Twitter, Facebook and LinkedIn. And for giving the new guy a chance. I'm especially thankful to Susan Joyce of JobHunt.org, Jacob Share of JobMob and Jason Alba of JibberJobber for their time and support.

Most important, thanks to all of you smart and talented job seekers who have allowed my blog, videos, tweets, updates, books and tools to influence and help you. If you like my Facebook page, joined my LinkedIn group, follow on Twitter or receive my newsletter, thank you!

Finally, I mentioned* some other people or resources in the book and wanted to add another thanks with the hope that you will do a Google search and learn more about each:

P. 11 Look for a great book by Bob Buford called *Halftime: Changing Your Game Plan From Success To Significance.*

P. 39 One of my favorite marketing books by Ries and Trout called *Positioning: The Battle For Your Mind.*

P. 47 Here I reference a great resource on Quintessential Careers website (http://www.quintcareers.com) about finding great action verbs for your resume.

P. 68-69 I share the blog of Kevin Liebl (http://kevinliebl.com) as a way to build influence on line with your subject matter expertise. Kevin's is marketing.

P. 70 I told you about Sven Johnston and his effort to get recognition for Orange County, CA on LinkedIn. His We Are OC group can be found on LinkedIn.

P.76 I mention Rick Warren of Saddleback Church, his book *The Purpose Driven Life* and the awesome career ministry that runs out of that church.

P. 83 I mention Steve Saccone who wrote *Relational Intelligence: How Leaders Can Expand Their Influence Through a New Way of Being Smart*. He provides a great platform for compassionate communication.

P. 91 If you read the chapter on talking to strangers, you'll know the story of how The Recruiting Animal led me from embarrassment to productivity via his radio show (http://www.blogtalkradio.com/animal).

Page 92 I mention a piece of advice from Bill Boorman (http://twitter.com/billboorman) who is a consultant to recruiters, helper to job seekers and organizer of #tru events a series of global recruiting "Unconferences".

Page 92 I mention Ryon Harms who writes a blog called The Social Executive (http://thesocialexecutive.com). Ryon helps individuals and businesses use social media productively.

Page 102 I include a mention of the Marketing Executives Networking Group (MENG), a national industry group for marketers (http://mengonline.com).

Page 149 I mention some smart people with great personal branding. Be sure to check out Dan Schawbel, Ryan Rancatore, Thom Singer, Meg Guiseppi, and Neal Schaffer.

Page 153-154 I mention a great article in *Scientific American Mind* by Trisha Gura called "I'll Do It Tomorrow". Trisha provides great tips from William Knaus on how to recognize when you are procrastinating.

---

* The mentions above in no way indicate an endorsement on their part of this book. I simply wanted to share some stories of people or resources that inspired me.

To learn more about
Tim Tyrell-Smith
and his Ideas for Job Search,
Career and Life, go to:

http://timsstrategy.com

Other books
from Tim Tyrell-Smith*

10 tools
The Tools Of Intelligent Job Search

I Can See Clearly Now
The Benefits of Taking Action on Your Ideas

*available as an ebook via timsstrategy.com

CPSIA information can be obtained at www.ICGtesting.com
Printed in the USA
236339LV00001B/212/P